In *Becoming God's Special Woman*, Jo Berry shows you how to develop self-worth. Through practical strategies, relevant anecdotes, and solid Bible teaching, she helps you to recognize your strengths and weaknesses and accept yourself as God made you. Thoroughly in tune with where you are today, this guidebook will show you how to:

- *establish self-sufficiency and self-identity*
- *reach your potential through prayer and studying God's Word*
- *be an individual*
- *serve others willingly and confidently*
- *trust your problems and shortcomings to the Lord*
- *find the root causes of poor self-esteem*
- *enjoy self-love*
- *receive the abundant blessings God wants to bestow upon you day by day*
- *gain an appreciation of yourself by observing Jesus Christ's loving treatment of women*

By Jo Berry
The Happy Home Handbook
Becoming God's Special Woman

Becoming GOD'S Special WOMAN

Becoming GOD'S Special WOMAN

Jo Berry

Power Books

Fleming H. Revell Company
Old Tappan, New Jersey

Unless otherwise identified Scripture quotations are from the New American Standard Bible, © The Lockman Foundation 1960, 1962, 1963, 1968, 1971, 1972, 1973, 1975, 1977.

Scripture quotations identified NIV are from the HOLY BIBLE: NEW INTERNATIONAL VERSION. Copyright © 1978 by the International Bible Society. Used by permission of Zondervan Bible Publishers.

Scripture quotations identified KJV are from the King James Version of the Bible.

Scripture quotations identified AMPLIFIED are from the Amplified New Testament © The Lockman Foundation 1954–1958, and are used by permission.

Scripture quotations identified PHILLIPS are from THE NEW TESTAMENT IN MODERN ENGLISH, Revised Edition—J. B. Phillips, translator. © J. B. Phillips 1958, 1960, 1972. Used by permission of Macmillan Publishing Co., Inc.

Excerpt from WHAT WIVES WISH THEIR HUSBANDS KNEW ABOUT WOMEN by James Dobson used by permission of Tyndale House Publishers, Inc. © 1975.

Lines reprinted from "Myself" from THE COLLECTED VERSE OF EDGAR A. GUEST © 1934, used with permission of Contemporary Books, Inc., Chicago, IL.

Library of Congress Cataloging-in-Publication Data

Berry, Jo.
    Becoming God's special woman.

    1. Women—Religious life.   2. Women—Psychology.
I. Title.
BV4527.B458   1986   248.8'43   85-30126
ISBN 0-8007-5219-8

TO my dear friend,
Shirley,
for walking through the valley
of the shadow with me

CONTENTS

PART I **What Keeps You From Feeling Special?**   11

    Chapter 1—What Is This Thing Called Self?   12

    Chapter 2—Does God Want You to Have a Good Self-Image?   26

    Chapter 3—The Lies You Tell Yourself   41

PART II **Improving Your Self-Image**   63

    Chapter 4—Learning to Love Yourself   64

PART III **Cultivating Self-Esteem**   93

    Chapter 5—Pursuing Peace   94

    Chapter 6—Acquiring Self-Respect   111

Contents

Chapter   7—Be All That You Can Be   127
Chapter   8—Becoming Vulnerable   137

PART IV **Establishing a Self-Identity**   153
Chapter   9—This Is Me!   154
Chapter 10—What Do You Need?   162
Chapter 11—Developing Survival Skills   170
Chapter 12—Becoming Self-Sufficient   179

PART V **Self-Actualization: Becoming God's Special Woman**   189
Chapter 13—Getting God's Input
                Through Prayer   190
Chapter 14—Getting God's Input
                Through His Word   203
Afterword   223

Becoming GOD'S Special WOMAN

Part I

What Keeps You From Feeling Special?

Chapter One

What Is This Thing Called Self?

She caught the attention of every woman the moment she walked into the room. She was dressed elegantly and stylishly, yet simply, in a print tailored blouse and a beige gathered skirt that hit her shapely legs at mid-calf. She was wearing gold hoop earrings, a thin, gold, serpentine chain necklace, and an emerald ring. Her reddish brown hair softly framed her angular face and her makeup was so perfectly applied and understated that she didn't look as though she were wearing any. She was stunning.

Judith August is a well-known fashion model and beauty consultant. She was speaking to the group about how your self-image is reflected in the way you sit, walk, stand, dress, and talk. She began with an excellent slide presentation that included photographs of dozens of women who, through their appearance, made some very definite statements about themselves. She asked the women in the audience to call out words or phrases that capsulized their impressions of the type of image portrayed in each photograph.

The responses were interesting. "Innocent," "angelic," to the picture of the young blonde girl in a pinafore; "sexy," "slinky," to the woman in a black evening gown; "athletic," "sporty," to the one in shorts and a tee shirt, who was holding a tennis racket; "vamp," "seductress," to the one who had a twenties Theda Bara look, complete with rhinestone headband, short, bobbed hair, and a long cigarette holder. "Exhausted," "housewife," to the one who was leaning on a mop, dressed in jeans, with a scarf tied around her head; "executive," "secretary," to a lady wearing a business suit and carrying a briefcase; "wealthy," "pampered," to one who was stretched out on a chaise lounge by a huge swimming pool, sipping a tall glass of something.

We laughed when Judith ended the presentation with a photograph of herself with the caption THE REAL ME superimposed in a corner. Then she said, "I'm going to flip back through the slides very quickly, and I want you to see if you notice anything special about them."

Gradually, as I studied each photograph, I realized that Judith had posed for every one of them. With the help of wigs, makeup and clothing, she had so thoroughly transformed herself that none of us had realized she was depicting all of those different women. She had successfully portrayed dozens of images.

"My point is this," she explained. "Externally, with the right facade, we can become anyone, but not to our mind's eye. Ultimately, what matters is the way we see ourselves."

The Four Aspects of Self

If you are going to become the special woman God created you to be, you must be willing to cast off facades, look deep within, and honestly appraise yourself with your mind's eye. There are four major aspects of self you need to examine and understand before you can caption yourself THE REAL ME: *self-image*, which is the way you see yourself; *self-esteem*, which is how you feel about yourself and react to who and what you are; *self-identity*, which is the person you actually are—the real you; and *self-actualization*, the person you are capable of becoming.

I visualize these facets as stair steps. The bottom step, your self-image (the way you see yourself) affects your self-esteem (how you feel about yourself), which formulates the third step, your self-identity (the person you actually are at this moment), which leads to self-actualization.

Actualization is defined as "becoming real or authentic." Although commonly used as a psychological term by Abraham Maslow, who viewed self-actualization as the highest level on the scale of human needs, for you as a Christian it means becoming a woman who wants to reach your full potential, not merely so you can be happy or feel good about yourself, but so you can please God and glorify Him. I think of self-actualization, which we will analyze fully in another section of this book, as becoming all God meant you to be—His special woman in the fullest sense.

Ideally, the easiest and best way to unearth the "real" you would be to start at point A and develop a realistic self-image, then to progress to point B and build a sense of self-worth, and then go to point C and establish your self-identity. Unfortunately, becoming God's special woman isn't quite that simple because life doesn't evolve in a neat, orderly progression. It seems to happen in unrelated clusters of activity and events. Consequently, by the time you're wise enough and mature enough to recognize deficiencies in your self-image, it is already largely established. So, becoming all God meant you to be is not like climbing stairs, where you start at the bottom and put one foot in front of the other until you reach the top. It's more like a child playing on a staircase, hopping from one step to another, skipping some, lingering on others. None of these facets of self is an absolute from which you progress methodically from point A to point B because each one of you is always in a state of flux. Some aspects of self are well developed, others are underdeveloped. Frequently, you end up straddling the stairs rather than taking orderly, decisive steps toward self-actualization.

The Way You See Yourself

I remember a student trainee who was assigned to my classroom when I was a training teacher for the Los Angeles City schools. She was a highly intelligent, sensitive young woman who, as she put it, "absolutely adored children." She was an only child as were both of her parents, so she had no brothers or sisters, no nieces and nephews. To compensate for the lack, she told me she intended to look at her students as part of the family she would never have. She was utterly convinced that she would make a marvelous teacher.

Sadly, as much as she liked children, she was a disaster with them in a formal classroom setting. She was so disorganized that she couldn't make lesson plans and so busy being a "buddy" to the children that she neglected the more important things like teaching reading, language, and arithmetic, and instilling self-discipline. My principal and I spent many hours trying to help her but ultimately we had to tell her there was no way we could recommend her for a credential.

She was dumbfounded. She had such a firm image of herself as a teacher that we had a great deal of difficulty convincing her she simply wasn't qualified for the job. She had misrepresented herself to herself. Her erroneous perspective of self was keeping her from becoming self-actualized.

That kind of imbalance can hamper any woman's development because your self-image (the way you see yourself) affects every aspect of your life, from the kind of clothing you wear and the kind of food you eat to the type of profession or friends you choose. You have feelings about and respond to the mental pictures you project *of* yourself *to* yourself. You look at the mental image, say, "This is me," and perform accordingly. The problem is, that image may or may not be accurate. You may have a distorted or unrealistic view of who and what you are. Many people misrepresent themselves to themselves, just as my teaching associate did. One way we can avoid this problem is to understand what our self-image is.

A Reflection of Self

The Proverbs describe self-image as the way our heart reflects us to ourselves: "As in water face reflects face, So the heart of man reflects man" (Proverbs 27:19). William M. Thackeray said self-image is "a looking glass and gives back to every man the reflection of his own face." Several years ago I had a lighted makeup mirror that could be adjusted to simulate various kinds of light: bright or overcast daylight, dusk and night, natural and artificial. The instructions said, when applying makeup, to choose the setting that most closely resembled the kind of light you'd be in. Since I worked in a room with fluorescent lighting, I usually used the bright, daylight setting, but it was harsh and unflattering and exposed every flaw. I knew if I ended up looking decent in that light, I'd done a good job of applying my makeup.

The dusk setting, however, treated me more kindly, rather like candlelight. Even without makeup, my skin had a rosy glow and looked soft. That setting distorted the reflection in my favor and made me look good, even when I didn't.

Like that makeup mirror, the mirror of self, which is the human heart, can deceptively shade reality. Sometimes it distorts the reflection in your favor; sometimes it is unnecessarily harsh and unjust in its assessment. The prophet Jeremiah warned, "The heart is more deceitful than all else and is desperately sick" (Jeremiah 17:9). Usually, self-image is a combination of fantasy and fact. Most of you know yourselves well in some ways, yet are constantly discovering new things and facing new realities about who and what you are. Part of becoming God's special woman involves learning to appraise yourself properly and look at yourself realistically, unearthing the "real" person beneath the obvious exterior.

Self-Esteem: *How You Feel About Yourself*

Whether your self-image is accurate or not, truthful or erroneous, you respond emotionally to the person you *think* you are. Those feelings you have about yourself form your self-esteem. Have you ever thought about how you react to who you are? In what ways do you like, respect and approve of yourself? Do certain characteristics make you angry at, critical of, and displeased with yourself? Generally, if you look at yourself and don't like what you see, you won't like yourself much, and you'll end up with a low sense of self-esteem.

I remember several years ago I was feeling lousy about myself because I'd gained twenty-five unwanted, unneeded, unflattering pounds. I didn't just dislike how I looked, my entire self-image suffered because I knew that the fat that had attached itself so firmly and stubbornly to my frame had gotten there because I wasn't mentally disciplined toward food, especially sweets. But I wasn't merely eating the wrong kinds of foods; I was overeating and consuming many more calories than I needed, because I was emotionally upset. I was upset because I had a problem I couldn't, or wouldn't, turn over to the Lord. I didn't like myself very much.

Finally, when I couldn't stand living with the fat, flabby, weak-willed person of little faith I'd become, I decided to do something about it. I wanted to feel good about myself again, so I joined a health spa. An instructor held a private consultation with each new member and set up a personalized exercise and diet program. Mine—you guessed it—excluded *all* sweets. I had to eliminate all sugar.

Then the instructor asked all nine of us women who joined the gym at the same time to get dressed in leotards so we could weigh in and be measured. Have you ever noticed how absolutely nobody in television ads for gyms and spas has an extra ounce of flesh on them? That certainly wasn't the case with our group. I've never seen such an assortment of shapes and sizes, and each fell far short of perfection.

After that humiliating experience, which made me think I should change my name to "Blimp" Berry, the instructor had us stand and study our bodies in the floor-to-ceiling mirror that covered one wall in the exercise room. "Look at yourselves as you are now," she suggested, "and decide what you want to see when you look in this same mirror six months from now. Make that your goal."

Let me tell you, I suffered; through hunger pangs, cravings, chocoholic fits, and sore muscles. But as the pounds and inches started melting away and I stopped looking and feeling like an overstuffed sausage when I put on my clothes, my self-esteem rose. Exercising regularly relieved stress, which helped me relax enough to be able to turn the problem that was plaguing me over to the Lord, which dissipated my urge to overeat. Six months later, when people were commenting about how much weight I'd lost and how much calmer I seemed, I decided I could approve of myself again.

Everyone Needs Self-Approval

Mark Twain said, "A man cannot be comfortable without his own approval." He called the hunger for self-approval the "Master Passion." Negating the need for self-affirmation is impossible because you have to live with yourself. You need to follow the advice of journalist Bill Copeland and learn to "be like a turtle—at ease in your own shell."

Denying the need for self-approval is foolish because if you don't validate yourself, you rely on others to do it for you. Then, if they can't or won't, you lose self-esteem and become even more disapproving of yourself. The best way to develop self-approval is to work constantly at becoming the woman God intended you to be. Dr. Archibald Hart advises that to unleash yourself from the shackles of self-hate you must "realistically recognize where you are *now* . . . You must move yourself to the place of accepting without resentfulness what you cannot change, and knowing where you stand on those aspects that can be changed" (*Feeling Free*, Revell, 1978, p. 129).

You need to follow the procedure my gym instructor gave. You need to look at yourself as you are now, not just physically but mentally, emotionally, and spiritually, and decide what you want to see and how you want to feel about yourself when you look into the mirror of self. Then you need to make raising your self-esteem one of your goals, realizing that it is a means to an end—a step up the stairs toward self-actualization and becoming God's special woman.

"Other" Approval Matters, Too

It's important to acknowledge that the opinion of others can have an effect on your self-esteem, too. Their input and reactions can make you feel good or bad about yourself. Egos are so fragile that a simple remark like, "Aren't you feeling well?" can generate negative emotions, even when you're feeling satisfied with yourself.

I recently heard a humorous story about a woman who decided to change her image. She had always worn rather drab colors—grays, blacks, and beiges—so she decided to buy a bright yellow dress. She wore it to church the following Sunday. She was happy and quite pleased with the way she looked and could hardly wait to see how other people would react. Her step had a lilt to it as she walked across the patio. The first person she encountered registered surprise, studied her intently, then said, "You certainly look *different.*" The next friend she met looked puzzled and asked, "Have you been sick?" The next, "Aren't you feeling well?" Another stopped her outside the sanctuary and whispered, "I wish you'd have let me know you'd been sick so I could have been praying for you." The poor woman's shoulders were stooped as she dragged into church and slumped into a pew, once again feeling dull and drab, convinced she looked awful and was coming down with the flu.

There is no doubt that your emotions affect your sense of self-esteem. In an article titled "Can Your Emotions Kill You?" which was published in *Psychology Today,* November, 1977, Dr. George Engel reported that a pronounced lack or loss of self-esteem can actually kill a person. A study he conducted showed that some cases of sudden death occur "in the wake of disappointment, failure, defeat, loss of status and self-esteem."

We see this happen frequently, when a couple has been married for many years and one dies; the other doesn't live long either. Experts believe this is because the widower or widow has lost his or her primary source of self-esteem.

The "You" That Stands Alone

Ultimately, the way you see yourself and feel about yourself formulates the person you become, or your self-identity. Some people become so dependent on others that their total identity is generated by their roles and relationships; they never become individuals in their own right. Everyone needs a self-identity, a "you" that stands alone, apart from all other people, because sooner or later in life each of us ends up in some situation where we're totally alone, where self is all we have.

For me, that happened sooner. When I was thirteen my mother was killed in an automobile accident; my father died exactly one year later. Abruptly, catastrophically, I was completely alone, forced to live with a guardian who, by today's enlightened standards would have been labeled abusive, alienated by him and his wife from my two brothers and their families. I was totally without any support system but myself and the Lord. Sometimes today I look back at that poor, naive, innocent little girl and am amazed that she survived. But by the grace of God, and with the help of a few good friends, she did.

I was fortunate because my parents had given me the gift of self. They had, in the way they raised me, taught me, even at that young age, that I was a person in my own right and that I was of great value to them, to God, and to myself. Reflecting back, I don't think that I knew who I was at that time, but I realized that I had certain capabilities and talents and I possessed a strong will to survive, against all odds. I was determined not to let anyone break me or make me into someone I didn't want to be. Through the years I have thanked the Lord many times that, through loving Christian parents and my faith in Him, He had established my self-identity so early in my life. I could not have survived without it.

You cannot grow into a healthy, whole, productive woman without a self-identity. You cannot become that authentic woman God created to be until, with His help, you get to know yourself well enough to say, "This is the *real* me."

Workshop

What Is This Thing Called Self?

I. In this chapter we defined *self-image* as the way you see yourself. This exercise will help you appraise your self-image. Take a moment to reflect on the woman you see when you look into the mirror of self. What do you admire about her? What qualities do you find unattractive? How are you different now from the way you were five years ago, a year ago, last month? Now, in the space below, write a brief description of the way you presently see yourself. When you finish, put a check by each quality you believe is an accurate appraisal. (Try to be objective. Don't be too hard on yourself. And remember that we all have erroneous ideas about ourselves, and you're trying to uncover some.) Finally, read the list to someone you trust and ask her what she believes is accurate and what is not.

_____

_____

_____

_____

_____

_____

II. We defined *self-esteem* as the feelings you have about yourself and the way you react to the person you are. This exercise will help you analyze how you feel about yourself and why. On the chart below, in the first column, list six of your most predominant personality and character traits. In the second column write a phrase describing how you feel about that trait and explain why you feel as you do. An example has been done for you.

Trait	Feeling and Reaction
EXAMPLE: *Determination*	*I have mixed emotions about this. Sometimes I like my determination because it helps me accomplish things. I am known as a reliable person who gets things done and that makes me feel good about myself. But sometimes my determination turns to stubbornness and that causes me problems.*
1.	
2.	
3.	
4.	
5.	
6.	

III. We defined *self-identity* as the woman you actually are. This exercise will help you assess your sense of identity. First, write the names of the significant people in your life under the appropriate category. Then, on a scale of 1 to 10, 10 being greatest, rate the impact you think each person has on your sense of identity. When evaluating, consider how much you rely on that person for emotional support and advice, how much you are affected by his or her opinions, and how efficiently you can function without his or her input.

Next, evaluate your findings. What might too many 9s or 10s mean? What might too many 1s or 2s indicate? If you gave 8s, 9s, or 10s to people who do not play a vital, ongoing role in your life, what might that tell you about how dependent you are on others for your sense of identity?

Immediate family	Extended family	Close friends
Neighbors	Acquaintances	
Business Associates	Other	

Chapter Two

―◦―

Does God Want You to Have a Good Self-Image?

Now that we've defined the four aspects of self, you may be reacting the way Sharon did when she spoke to me after a seminar. She said, "Of course I *want* to improve my self-image and feel better about myself, but I don't know where to begin. Just where and how do I start becoming God's special woman?"

That's an important and necessary question. Your inclination will be to start by looking at yourself and deciding what's wrong and what you want to change. That's what most experts advise. They suggest that we examine ourselves, isolate and analyze our problems, then do whatever is necessary to solve them, even at the expense of hurting or belittling others.

An article I read in a popular woman's magazine suggested that we should "put down" everyone who says or does anything that diminishes our self-esteem. If your husband criticizes your cooking, point out that he's not so great at fixing faucets. If a friend gets on your case for not returning her phone call, remind her of a time she neglected you. In other words, build yourself up by tearing down others.

The Problem With a "Self" Centered Approach

I disagree with that kind of "self" centered approach for several reasons. One is that belittling or hurting others doesn't make you feel better about yourself; it makes you feel worse. Another is that it creates an imbalance in your relationships. You can get so absorbed in yourself that you neglect God and others. You become a human sponge, who only soaks up self. I keep a big, yellow sponge handy in my kitchen to wipe up spills. I used it the other day when my daughter accidentally kicked over the cat's milk. I put the sponge on the puddle of milk, and it soaked up every drop. The sponge didn't change. It was still big and yellow and rectangular, but it was full of the milk it had absorbed. Centering on yourself rather than God doesn't change you any more than absorbing the milk changed that sponge. All self-absorption does is make you full of self; it doesn't change your self-image for the better.

The main reason I object to the "self" centered approach is that it focuses us on ourselves (the problem) rather than God (who holds the solution to the problem). You can't love yourself unconditionally, but He can, so He can nudge you toward self-acceptance by helping you learn how to love yourself. Most of you aren't capable of analyzing yourselves objectively but He is, so He can reveal you to yourselves as you really are and show each of you how to become an authentic, godly woman. He can teach you how to develop self-worth His way, how to raise your self-esteem without hurting or devaluing anyone. As contradictory as it may sound, the only way to make permanent, positive changes in your self-image is to start by focusing on the Lord rather than on yourself.

To do this, you need to learn and use some basic biblical principles about self-image, because you may have some major misconceptions about the topic.

I unearthed some the first time I taught a six-week Bible study about self-image. Before the first lesson I asked the women to break into groups of three or four and discuss this statement: I believe God wants me to have a good self-image because. . . . When they shared their responses, I was astonished to find that at least three-fourths of the women weren't sure God *did* want them to have a good self-image. Some said they thought that thinking about yourself is selfish. Others said they thought we were supposed to "keep our eyes on Jesus," not ourselves. One woman said, "I don't think God *does* want me to have a good self-image or He wouldn't let so many things happen to me that make me feel so lousy about myself." Another shared that she believed the topic of self-image is a worldly concept that isn't talked about in the Bible, so it shouldn't be taught in the church. Their replies indicated that I certainly had my work cut out for me, because many of them didn't believe that God wants us to have a good self-image.

In His Image

Let's examine four biblical principles that can clarify some of those common misconceptions and help you understand that God *does* want each of you to have a good self-image.

The first is: *You are created in the image of God.* Genesis 1:27 says, "God created man in His own image, in the image of God He created him; male and female He created them." As you read through the creation story, you'll discover that plants and animals are created after their own kind: roses are like roses and dogs are like dogs, but human beings— the most special of all God's creation—are made "according to [God's] likeness" (Genesis 1:26).

Being created in the image of God doesn't mean you look like Him; it means you *are* like Him. God is a Person. God has emotions; you have feelings. He is creative; you have ambition. He is a sovereign, self-determining individual; He created you with a will and the ability to choose. God has an intellect; He thinks and reasons, therefore, so can you. He is totally unique; there is no other god like Him. Each person He created is totally unique. There never has been and never will be another woman exactly like you. All of these human traits are the result of your being created in the image of God. They are characteristics we do not see in animals or plants.

To improve self-image, you need to look for and appreciate your godliness.

For example, Evelyn is a tenderhearted, sensitive woman who has a tremendous capacity for identifying with the pain and suffering of others. She offers more than a shoulder to cry on; she literally sorrows and cries with you and for you. But for years, Evelyn was embarrassed by her ready tears and by what she thought was an inability to control her emotions. I once heard her tell someone she wished she could be stronger. This misinterpretation detracted from her self-image.

Then, when Evelyn's pastor preached a series on spiritual gifts, she realized that she wasn't weak or merely an overly emotional female but that she had the gift of mercy. Her tears, her caring, her concern, were part of God's image that He had woven into the fiber of her being. She has come to accept and appreciate those characteristics as part of her Godlikeness; His mercy reflected through her humanity.

An old adage notes that imitation is the sincerest form of

flattery. That Almighty God, creator of the universe, chose, in His sovereign wisdom and love, to make each of you miniature reproductions of His likeness should help you see yourself in a positive way. It should help you accept yourself and instill in you an attitude of gratitude.

Be Grateful You're You

That's the next biblical self-image principle: *You should be grateful to God for who and what you are.* In Psalm 139 David praised God because he was fearfully and wonderfully made (v. 14). *Fearfully* means "fashioned with reverence and respect," implying that when God created you He did it thoughtfully and with careful consideration to detail.

Job 10:8 says, "Thy hands fashioned and made me altogether." I heard a leading designer explain on a television talk show how he fashions an article of clothing. He said he makes numerous sketches, until the garment he's designing is exactly to his liking. Next, he decides what color to use; then selects the perfect fabric to convey the effect he's after. After he makes the final sketch, a member of his staff makes a pattern, which he then alters to suit his taste further. Once the basic pattern is precisely as he likes, a seamstress constructs a trial garment, which he again alters until it is perfect, according to his standards. Then he closely inspects the finished article of clothing, makes final design changes and adjustments before the final product is sewn. He stressed that he closely supervises every step because he wants the finished garment to turn out exactly as he fashioned it. He said, "I want every little detail to be absolutely perfect."

The Lord fashions each person He creates with reverence and respect that far exceeds that of any human designer. He makes every little detail about us perfect, according to His specifications. David realized that when he said, "I am fearfully and wonderfully made."

David displayed an attitude of gratitude about who and what he was. He said, "Wonderful are Thy works, And my soul knows it very well" (Psalms 139:14). *Wonderful* means "awesome and amazing." But David wasn't being egotistical when he praised God. He wasn't saying, "Wow, Lord, when You made me, You really outdid Yourself!" He was acknowledging that in his heart he was willing to accept himself, just as God made him. Even though he had faults. Even though he had some hurtful ways about him. Even though there were things he didn't like about himself. Even though he sometimes hated the way he acted, he was still grateful to the Lord for the way He created him.

Scripture teaches that everything God created was good. When you degrade or devalue yourself, you are demeaning an awesome, amazing work God performed with reverence and respect. That kind of ingratitude is a sin because it implies that God, who is infallible, made a mistake. And it may seem like He did, from your limited point of view, but not from His.

When I was a girl, there was a spinster named Alma who attended our church. She was one of the homeliest people I'd ever seen. She was at least six feet tall and extremely skinny. Her nose was flattened wide against her face and her eyes were close-set and round like an owl's. One of her ears was deformed, and she had a harelip that caused a slight speech impediment. She played the piano in my Sunday-school department, and I remember I always looked away quickly whenever our eyes met.

In spite of all those surface defects, Alma was one of the happiest people I've ever known. She was always smiling and humming and was friendly and kind to everyone, even bratty kids like me who laughed at her behind her back and called her "Ugly Alma." When she died, my parents made me go with them to her funeral. Although I don't remember his exact words, I've never forgotten something the pastor said. He said that Alma was a woman who never complained, although according to most of us, she had three strikes against her when she was born. She was, he said, beautiful inside, so she was able to accept the way God had clothed her soul.

Alma's faith and acceptance of the way God fashioned her had made her whole. Her example proves that once you are willing to accept yourself, just as you are, you can be grateful to God for who and what you are.

Love Yourself

When you do, you're able to apply the next scriptural self-image principle: *It is God's will that you love yourself.* First John 4:19 says, "We love, because He first loved us." Once we accept God's love, in the Person of His Son, we are then capable of loving ourselves, God, and others. The apostle John wrote that ". . . love is from God . . ." (1 John 4:7), and I believe that includes self-love.

Legitimate self-love is inspired by God. For some reason many people, especially Christians, assume that thinking about yourself and acknowledging that you have worth is sinfully egotistical. Egotism, which is self-inspired love that is blind to faults and exalts self above God and others *is* a sin, but loving and appreciating yourself is not. "It is not love of self, but love of self alone, which is sinful" (Lewis B. Smedes, *Mere Morality*, Eerdmans, 1983, p. 52).

There's a vast difference between egotism and legitimate love of self. Contrast Mohammed Ali's arrogant proclamation, "I'm the greatest!" with Paul's affirmation of self in 1 Corinthians 15:10: "By the grace of God I am what I am, and His grace toward me did not prove vain. . . ." One is the height of ego; the other a manifestation of God-inspired self-love.

God wants you to love yourself because it's difficult, if

not impossible, to love anyone else if you don't. It's a fact of life that you cannot pass on to others attributes you don't possess. A wife who doesn't love herself isn't free to love her husband unconditionally. A mother who has a low opinion of herself can't instill self-esteem in her child. A woman who is unjustly critical of herself because she doesn't love herself will also be unfairly critical of her colleagues, neighbors, and family. Lack of self-love hurts everyone, not just the individual. Dr. James Dobson observed, "Personal worth is not something human beings are free to take or leave. We must have it and when it is unattainable, everybody suffers" (*Hide or Seek*, Revell, 1974, p. 13).

A legitimate love of self starts when you accept that you have value. I've noticed that Christians have a tendency to confuse unworthiness with worthlessness. *Unworthy* is defined as "not deserving of merit," and *worthless* as "without worth or value." Certainly, none of us deserves God's grace, unmerited love, and favor. In that respect we *are* unworthy. *But each of us is of value to God!* "God so greatly loved and dearly prized (valued) the world that He [even] gave up His only-begotten (unique) Son . . ." (John 3:16 AMPLIFIED).

Christ's earthly ministry pointed up our unworthiness but at the same time validated our worth. Every person with whom He came in contact paled by comparison—His holiness magnified our sinfulness—yet, His compassionate response to their individual needs and problems illustrates how much He valued each imperfect person. An unclean leper came to Him and said, "If You are willing, You can make me clean" (Mark 1:40), and He was willing to touch and heal him. A short, hated, dishonest tax collector named Zaccheus needed a friend, and Christ was willing to trust him. Mary Magdalene, who had seven demons; Martha, whose heart was broken because her beloved brother, Lazarus, had died; Peter who denied Him; Judas, who betrayed Him; James and John who insulted and misunderstood Him; the woman with an issue of blood, who needed to be healed; the woman at the well who desperately needed to have her self-esteem restored: each needed Him in a special way, and He was willing and accepted them and loved them, never demanding worthiness. Instead, He motivated and encouraged them toward repentance.

It *is* God's will that you love and value yourself because He does. If He thinks you're worth loving, you are!

Have a Balanced Perspective of Self

But loving and accepting yourself doesn't mean that you can overlook your faults and failings. Another biblical principle about self-image is: *It is God's will that you maintain a balanced perspective of yourself.* That means you accept and appreciate the basic product He created but that you also acknowledge the imperfections caused by sin and self (the flesh). In his translation of the New Testament, J. B. Phillips refers to this ability to see both good and bad, and strengths and weaknesses as making a sane estimate of self. His paraphrase of Romans 12:3 reads, "Don't cherish exaggerated ideas of yourself or your importance but try to make a sane estimate of your capabilities by the light of faith that God has given to you all." That verse contains a biblical formula on how to maintain a God-honoring, balanced perspective of self.

Don't Cherish Exaggerated Ideas of Yourself

First, you're warned what *not* to do: "Don't cherish exaggerated ideas of yourself or your importance." These exaggerated ideas are opinions you have about yourself which go beyond what is factual or true. They may be either favorable or unfavorable, on the plus or minus side of truth, but they are ways you think wrongly about yourself.

I know a woman who, every time she shares an idea, prefaces it by saying, "I know this is probably stupid but. . . ." Despite the fact that her suggestions usually make sense, she has an exaggerated idea that her opinions aren't valid or intelligent.

I know another woman who thinks she has a beautiful singing voice. For years people have tried to tell her politely that she'd be great in the choir but that she just can't cut it as a soloist. Now she's talking about starting a recording company of her own because none of the producers she's sent demo tapes over the past ten years has recognized her potential.

Both of these women *cherish* exaggerated ideas of themselves. The word *cherish* means "to love and nurture." Each has embellished erroneous thoughts about herself over a long period of time and, in spite of evidence to the contrary, refuses to face the truth or turn loose of them. Consequently, they both have a distorted self-image: one thinks less of herself than she should; the other thinks more highly of herself that she ought. One debases and devalues herself; the other suffers from false pride. Neither has a balanced perspective of herself.

Make a Sane Estimate of Your Capabilities

Scripture offers a practical solution to the problem of exaggerated ideas. It instructs you to try to make a sane estimate of your capabilities, to assess realistically your good points and bad, your capabilities and limitations, character strengths and flaws, prevalent attitudes and overriding personality traits. You must try to see yourself as you actually are.

When I was on a plane last November, headed for Toronto to teach a self-image seiminar, an ad in the newspaper I was reading immediately caught my eye. Large, white letters set boldly against a black background asked WHO DO YOU THINK YOU ARE? A question mark three times the size of the heading was positioned over the sentence. The text of the ad asked, "Have you ever wondered who and what you really are? Have you pondered the nature of life and universe, and questioned why you do the things you do?"

Haven't we all? Who among us hasn't at one time or another asked that universal question, who am I? Making a sane estimate of your capabilities means repeatedly asking the question, so you can get to know yourself well enough to answer it honestly.

Years ago, when I took a fiction-writing course, one of the first things the instructor taught was that an author has to know the characters she's going to write about as well as she knows herself. He said, "If you don't know yourself, you won't be able to develop good characters." He explained that during the course we'd be required to develop character sketches of ten fictitious people we might want to include in the great American novel we all hoped to write someday. Then he gave the class an interesting assignment. We each had to write a biographical sketch about ourselves for our first project, pretending we were going to be the main character in that novel. He told us he wanted us to depict ourselves as real people, with warts as well as beauty marks.

He gave us a set of guidelines to use, which I still have. They were:

1. *Physical description. Include what the character does and does not like about the way he or she looks and other people's reactions to the way the person looks.*

2. *Basic philosophy of life. What is the character's value system? How does he or she think and respond? Morals?*
3. *Family background and environment. How did this person get to be the person he or she is? Include formulative people and events.*
4. *Personality traits. What is the character like?*
5. *Motivation. What makes the character behave as he or she does?*

I learned a lot about myself from doing that assignment, including some things I didn't know, or hadn't been willing to admit. Looking at myself in such a detailed, objective way, from a different perspective, helped me understand who I am and why I do what I do. You, too, can benefit from making that kind of honest appraisal of yourself.

The Light of Faith

But you can't make a sane estimate of your capabilities without God's help because you're blinded by the darkness of sin. You're like the people Isaiah described when he said, "You [feel] secure in your wickedness . . . Your wisdom and your knowledge, they have deluded you" (Isaiah 47:10). Because you are a sinner, wisdom and knowledge about yourself deludes you. You lie to yourself about yourself. You keep secrets from yourself about yourself. You reject truth. You may live as a stranger to self, never knowing yourself as you actually are. You simply are not capable of seeing yourself realistically without God's help. But when you ask Him to show you yourself from His perspective, "He who reveals the profound and hidden things; He knows what is in the darkness, And the light dwells with Him" (Daniel 2:22).

Some people don't want to see themselves as they really are, so they avoid the light, but in the end even a little light is better than darkness. And, it's much safer to walk in light than in darkness. Otherwise, you're always tripping and falling over some fault or mistake.

In a story I read about a man who was exploring and got lost in a cave, he said the most terrifying part of the experience was being engulfed in total darkness when his lantern burned out. He said he lost all sense of reality; he couldn't tell day from night or up from down. He imagined all sorts of creatures were after him and said he was certain he'd have gone insane if he hadn't been rescued when he was. He said the most beautiful sight he'd ever seen in his life was a tiny ray of light in the distance from the flashlight of a member of the rescue team as he approached.

When a news reporter asked what he'd learned from his frightening experience, he said that first of all he'd learned never to go exploring alone again. And, that he'd learned that it's better to face any reality, no matter how horrible it might be, than to be swallowed up in total darkness.

Scripture says you must assess yourself "by the light of the faith that God has given to you" (Romans 12:3 PHILLIPS). That light of faith can help you face realities about yourself and keeps you from being engulfed in the darkness of error. When you look at yourself through that "light of faith," God, who knows you far better than you know yourself, can show you yourself as you really are and help you make a sane estimate to self. And He gives you the faith and ability to believe in yourself, rather than clinging to erroneous, exaggerated ideas that debilitate your self-image.

Workshop

Does God Want You to Have a Good Self-Image?

I. In this chapter we established that we are created in the image of God. This exercise will help you identify some aspects of your Godlikeness. Look up each Scripture, list the attribute of God it describes, then write a sentence telling how you reflect that characteristic.

Scripture	Attribute of God	Reflection in Self
1. 1 John 4:16		
2. Psalms 36:5		
3. Psalms 145:17		
4. Psalms 103:8		
5. John 15:11		
6. Psalms 136:1–3		

II. Do you have an attitude of gratitude for who and what you are? Read and reflect on Psalms 139:13–16; then in the space below, list three ways in which you are fearfully and wonderfully made. Write a prayer thanking God for those attributes.

_____

_____

_____

III. In this chapter we established that it is God's will that we love ourselves. Look at some things Christ did that prove that is true. Read each Scripture then write two or three sentences explaining how Jesus showed He loved and accepted each person, just as they were. Next write a sentence describing what He did to encourage them toward repentance and valid self-love.

1. John 8:1–11
2. Mark 1:40–42
3. Mark 14:3–9
4. Luke 7:12–15
5. Luke 19:1–10

IV. In this chapter we learned that it is God's will that we maintain a balanced perspective of ourselves. Using the outline on pages 36 and 37, write a biographical sketch about yourself, pretending you are going to be the main character in a novel. (Be sure to include beauty marks as well as warts!)

Chapter Three

The Lies You Tell Yourself

There is no doubt that God can and wants to reveal the truth to you concerning who and what you are, but you cannot improve your self-worth unless you *want* to discover the truth about yourself. But many of you don't want to know the truth about yourselves even when you ask for it. You're like the woman in a cartoon I saw. It depicted an extremely angry wife, standing with her arms folded across her chest and her jaw set, glaring at her befuddled husband. She had apparently dumped a potted plant on his head because his face and shirt were covered with dirt and a drooping geranium blossom was sticking out of his left ear. The caption read, "But you said you wanted my honest opinion about your new hairdo."

One thing I've observed that keeps a lot of women from facing the truth and seeing themselves as beautiful in God's eyes, and their own, is the lies they tell themselves and live by. David said, "The Lord is near to all who call upon Him, To all who call upon Him in truth" (Psalms 145:18).

If you truly want to become God's special woman, you must be willing to ask God for His input, then to accept His honest opinion when He reveals the truth to you.

Lie Number One: "I Can't Change"

Let's look at some of the lies you may be telling yourself and see what you can do to discover the truth. The first lie you have to battle is: "I'm the way I am, and I can't change." Many people resist change. They're more comfortable with the known (who they presently are) than the unknown (what they might become within the will of God). Even if they're dissatisfied with themselves, they know what they are and feel safe with the status quo. An old German proverb notes, "An old error is always easier to live by than a new truth." Saying "That's how I am" is easier than changing, but is extremely detrimental to your self-worth.

I once heard the story about a caterpillar who watched a beautiful butterfly fluttering from leaf to leaf then sighed and said, "As bad as things are down here, you'd never get me up in that contraption." Many Christians think like that about themselves and their potential. They have no vision of what they can become in Christ, of the changes that are possible. They'd rather stay stuck with their old self-image, as warped as it might be, than to take God at His word.

You are lying to yourself if you believe you can't change. In fact, *once you are joined to Christ, you are no longer the same person you once were.* Leo Tolstoy said, "When I came to believe in Christ's teaching . . . the direction of my life . . . became different. What was good and bad changed places."

Tolstoy is right! He affirms Paul's well-known cry of joy that "if any man is in Christ, he is a new creature; the old things passed away; behold, new things have come"

(2 Corinthians 5:17). A lot of you may parrot what Paul wrote, but you don't make it part of your own experience. Instead of accepting and rejoicing in the change that Christ has brought, you keep telling yourself those debilitating, timeworn lies from which you've been set free. This detracts from your self-worth because it keeps you from discovering new truths. If you don't identify and eliminate those lies, you'll keep on believing that you really are as bad as you once imagined you were. Your self-image will stay distorted instead of realistic; your self-esteem will suffer.

Overcoming Resistance to Change

There are two things you must do to overcome resistance to change. The first is to *accept that you are already different.* What was once true about you doesn't have to be true any longer. You are no longer alone. You are joined with God! Jesus promised, ". . . I am in My Father, and you in Me, and I in you" (John 14:20). You are no longer powerless because you are no longer the way you were, so you should start thinking of yourself as a changing woman. In their book *Catch a Red Leaf*, Gladis and Gordon DePree observe: "When we see our lives as being infused with the life of God, there is nothing, no moment, no instance which is lived apart from God . . . we become different people. The change might or might not be sudden, but it is there" (Zondervan, 1980, p. 37).

The second way to overcome resistance to change is to *believe that God can change you.* He is in the people-changing business. With God's touch, Saul, the hateful executioner, became Paul, the apostle. Mary, the prostitute became Mary, the devoted disciple. The Christ who changed the water into wine is perfectly capable of transforming you.

The problem is, a lot of people don't let God change them. As I see it, we have three choices when it comes to deprogramming the "I'm the way I am and I can't change" lie.

You Can Deteriorate

One is, you can *deteriorate*, which means "to make or become worse." Some people choose to go back to the way they were before they became Christians, to repeat the same old sin patterns and live the same lies they lived before they were set free by the truth.

That's what happened to Vivian. She was in the midst of a divorce when she accepted Christ. Her self-esteem was almost nonexistent, which is understandable because her husband had left her for another woman who was much younger than she, and her three teenage children wanted to go live with their father and his new bride-to-be. As we talked, Vivian admitted that she'd gained thirty pounds from "nervous eating," that she wasn't taking proper care of herself or her home, that she had been drinking a bit to calm her nerves, and that she had constantly nagged and yelled at the kids and her husband. We discussed several approaches she could use to rebuild her relationship with her children and gain her self-respect.

She went on a diet, bought some new clothes, stopped drinking, and started fixing decent meals and doing laundry again. She apologized to each of her children and tried to open the emotionally clogged lines of communication with them. But, like so many women in her position, she felt she had to affirm her femininity by proving she could still attract a man, so she started going to singles bars with a woman from her office. Eventually, she was picking up men and engaging in casual sexual encounters. She also started drinking heavily and ignoring her children. She was behaving worse than she had before she became a Christian. Except, she was consumed by the guilt of her sin. Vivian chose to deteriorate, to slip backwards to a low point she'd never experienced before.

You Can Stagnate

A second choice you can make regarding change is that you can *stagnate*, which means "to become dull or inactive," and stay as you are. This means you don't get worse than you were before you received Christ, but you don't get any better. Immense, positive changes are possible once you are in Christ, but you can't change by conforming to what you've always been! You change by conforming to the image of Christ.

I was raised in Kansas, and as a little girl, I would go fishing with my dad. I loved playing in the creek, but he always warned me to stay out of the stagnant ponds that formed from the overflow. He said the water was contaminated because it didn't move. As I've taught Bible studies and seminars, and talked with hundreds of people who were convinced they couldn't change, I've often had occasion to remember my father's warning. Anytime you just stand and don't move, you're stagnating. But when Christ, the Living Water, comes in, He acts as a fresh, free-flowing stream of truth that washes away the old lies you've been telling yourself for years. But if you just sit and don't let Christ cleanse you with the truth, you stagnate.

When people choose to say, "This is how I am and I can't change," their Christianity doesn't have much effect on what they think or do. John W. Gardner, former Secretary of Health, Education and Welfare, and a man who is known for his keen observations about human nature, believes people stop learning and growing because they adopt fixed attitudes and opinions. He said, "Most of us, in fact, progressively narrow the scope and variety of our lives." That's stagnation! No new pathways! No fresh input!

You Can Grow New Wood

Are you doomed to be the way you are, as some people believe? Is deterioration or stagnation your fate? Of course not. You have another choice. You can *grow* new wood. That's what the famous poet Henry Wadsworth Longfellow recommended when he was once asked why he had such an optimistic outlook on life. He pointed to an apple tree on the hill and said, "The secret of that tree's productivity is that it grows a little new wood each year. That is what I plan to do."

One summer when my husband, George, and son, Brian, and I were hiking in Yosemite National Park, we came across a huge tree that we assumed had been felled by lightning. Although it retained some of its original shape, the core of the wood was rotten and full of all sorts of creepy, crawly critters and decay. Christians who don't grow "new wood" are like that tree; they either stagnate or deteriorate. But those who believe God can and has changed them grow "new wood." They progress toward the goal He intends—conformity to the image of His Son. They see themselves differently. They don't say, "I can't change"; they say, "I am changed!"

Lie Number Two: "I Can't Overcome the Past"

Another common lie people tell themselves is, *"I can't overcome the past."* Many adults blame most or all of their self-image problems on the past, sometimes rightly so. You are all, to varying extents, products of your environments. You have been molded, directed, and influenced by the people and events that have been a part of your life. The past, in many ways, shaped each of you into the person you are today. I know I wouldn't be nearly so independent nor self-reliant if I hadn't been orphaned when I was fourteen.

I had no choice but to fend for myself. I learned to do a lot of things for myself that I know my parents would have done for me had they lived. I lost a huge chunk of my childhood very fast. Being on my own at such an early age forced me to make major decisions and stand up for my beliefs. You've probably faced similar circumstances, whether pleasant or unpleasant.

Denying the impact the past has on you would be foolish, but so is wallowing in it, refusing to release it, or letting it control the present. You can't undo the past or change it, but you don't have to dwell on it or be victimized by it because being in Christ helps you overcome the effect of the past. God doesn't change or erase the past, but He can lead you beyond it, to the place where it is no longer a formulative factor in your life, your relationships, or the future, unless you let it be.

I know two sisters, whom I'll call Andrea and Deborah. Their father was an alcoholic, their mother all but ignored them because she didn't want the responsibility of raising them. She was so involved in her own life and pain while they were growing up, including having several affairs, that she never taught them any of the normal things mothers teach their daughters, such as how to choose clothes, put on makeup, select friends, or cook a decent meal. But she expected them to keep house for the family from the time they were four and six years old.

When they were in the fifth and seventh grades, their older brother started sexually molesting them and threatened to have his buddies rape them if they told. This coercion of fear continued through high school. The only thing that kept both girls sane was their love for each other and their determination to get out of their situation.

When Andrea graduated, she immediately left home and held down three jobs while attending a junior college. She wanted to be a nurse. Their parents were pleased when she asked if Deborah could move in with her. Both girls were relieved to get away from their home, but spent a lot of time planning how to get even with their family. They were bent on revenge, motivated by the hatred, anger, and bitterness that had accumulated in their hearts through the years. They decided to write a journal, detailing everything their parents and brother had done to them, then to turn their family over to the police once Deborah turned eighteen. They spent most of their spare time recording all of the horrible physical and emotional indignities they had suffered.

Then a girl Andrea met in one of her classes invited her to a Bible study. Shortly after that, Andrea accepted Christ. When she started going to church, reading the Bible, and fellowshiping with Christians, she spent less and less time writing the journal with Deborah. She tried to get her sister to go to Sunday school with her, but Deborah got angry at Andrea and said that God was taking her sister away from her. Deborah felt betrayed.

As soon as Deborah graduated from high school, she got a job as a barmaid, so she could get an apartment of her own. She was furious because Andrea no longer wanted to go to the authorites and turn in her parents and brother. Instead, Andrea wanted to try to reach out to them in love.

Andrea was torn when she came to talk with me. She said she'd tried to reason with Deborah, but that she wouldn't listen. She was concerned because Deborah was totally consumed with getting even. "She's messing up her whole future," Andrea sobbed, "because of something that happened in the past. She thinks our family ruined her life, but they didn't. She's ruining it herself." Then she said something I've thought about so often: "She can't understand that the past just doesn't matter to me anymore now that I have Jesus."

The last I heard, Deborah had dropped out of sight and abandoned all family ties and Andrea had married a fine Christian man. Sadly, Deborah chose to let the past dictate her future, but Andrea trusted God to lead her beyond all of the past hurt and humiliation.

The fact that the past just doesn't have to matter anymore, once you have Jesus, can apply to you if you'll let it. In his column in the *Los Angeles Times* (February 17, 1985) Leo F. Buscaglia commented, ". . . many of us find it convenient to assign responsibility for our behavior to someone in our formative past. No matter how much of a cushion it provides for our present self-image, it does little to help in getting on with life and coming to terms with our problems."

I can hear some of you saying, "That's easy for you to suggest, but you don't know what I've been through." That's true. I don't, nor do you know what I've been through either. But I do know God has brought us out on the other side of yesterday into the present and is ushering us toward the future. I'm not claiming that overcoming the past is easy, but it is possible. I wish I had a simple formula to tell you how to do that, but I don't. I do, however, know what's worked for me, and I pass those principles on to you.

Principles for Overcoming the Past

Leave the past with God. Literally turn it over to Him, once and for all. Dwelling on negative portions of the past is debilitating and never makes you feel good about yourself. It conjures up all sorts of sinful feelings: guilt, anger, bitterness, inadequacy, helplessness. Instead of thinking about the past, put it in His hands and ask Him to use it for His glory and your betterment. In Romans 8:28, Paul declared that "God causes all things to work together for good to those who love God . . ." and that *all* includes your past. Visualize yourself putting it in a box, along with all its accompanying feelings, and handing it to Jesus Christ. Ask Him to bring good from it, then trust that He will.

Force yourself to dwell on the present. Every time your thoughts slip back into the negative past or you start replaying unpleasant scenarios in your mind, do something to distract yourself. This requires mental discipline and an act of your will. Refuse to look back. Think about now. Make plans for today. Talk to yourself. Read a book. Take a walk or phone a friend. Do errands. Pray and read Scripture. Weed the garden. Write a letter. Sing a hymn. Count your blessings. Name them aloud, one by one, and thank God for them.

Accept responsibility for the present. In their book, *Catch a Red Leaf*, Gladis and Gordon DePree observed: "Although I am influenced by those who came before me . . . I cannot draw my strength from anyone else or blame my weaknesses on anyone other than myself" (Zondervan, 1980, p. 55).

Are you excusing your present faults, failings, and bad behavior by blaming the past? You need to stop lying, telling yourself that you can't overcome the past. Instead, you must concentrate on learning new truths about the Lord and yourself. Tomorrow, today will be a part of the past. Today well lived means you can look with favor on yesterday and feel good about your part in it.

If necessary, seek counsel. You may need to talk through the past with a trained, competent adviser, such as a pastor, skilled lay counselor or a Christian psychologist. Verbalizing will help you identify, confess, and deal with those old-self hangovers in a God-honoring way. It will also help you learn the truth.

Keep telling yourself the truth. Every time you start believing that you can't overcome the past, tell yourself that in Christ, you can do all things.

Lie Number Three: "It's All My Fault"

A third lie you may be telling yourself is, "It's all my fault." Instead of blaming the past and others, some people blame themselves for every negative thing that happens, or ever has happened, in their lives. They assume huge portions of unnecessary guilt. Saying "it's all my fault" is just another way of saying, "I'm a lousy person who's capable of causing all kinds of problems."

Actually, there are two kinds of guilt: legitimate and illegitimate. Legitimate guilt is real. It is the uneasiness of conscience and conviction of the Holy Spirit you experience when you sin. You deal with legitimate guilt through confession and repentance.

Illegitimate guilt is imagined and stems from a weird sort of pride. Some people think so little of themselves that they unreasonably, unfairly, and illogically assume they have the power to provoke negative results in all sorts of situations. They draw attention to themselves and receive recognition by saying, "It's all my fault."

Myrna was like that. When her son broke his arm playing baseball, it was because she let him join the team. When her husband was in an automobile accident, it was because she traded cars with him that day. When she was chairperson of the women's fellowship group at her church and a fund-raising banquet fell short of its goal, it was her fault because she hadn't personally sold enough tickets. Most of Myrna's guilt was a product of her imagination. It wasn't real. She desperately wanted to matter to people and have an effect in their lives, but because she thought she had nothing positive to contribute, like a child who misbehaves to get attention, she took credit for all the negatives.

The truth is ... *Christ negated your guilt on the cross.* Paul proclaimed, "There is therefore now no condemnation for those who are in Christ Jesus" (Romans 8:1). The Saviour bore your guilt so you wouldn't have to. He suffered rejection and condemnation so you could be accepted and commended. Assuming unwarranted guilt doesn't merely detract from your feelings of self-worth; it insults Christ's finished work in your life. Claiming you're guilty when you're not is as wrong as saying you aren't guilty when you are.

Principles for Deprogramming Guilt

If you're a "Myrna" who has a tendency to say, "It's all my fault," practicing these principles can help you deprogram illegitimate guilt.

Forgive yourself. God has. "When you were dead in your transgressions ... He made you alive together with Him, having forgiven us all our transgressions" (Colossians 2:13). Many people who have a poor self-image have difficulty accepting positive truths about themselves, including the fact that God has forgiven and accepted them in Christ. You must remember that Jesus said *all* unforgiveness is a sin (Matthew 6:14, 15) and that includes harboring ill will or malice toward yourself. You need to follow the Lord's injunction to forgive your debtors, including any grudges you're holding against yourself. Forgiving past debts means that no matter how much in the red anyone is, or imagines himself or herself to be, once you are *in* Christ, you can wipe the books clean and start a new ledger—one that's stamped PAID IN FULL and signed with Christ's blood. As the hymn says, "Jesus paid it all." He died for your sins, past, present and future, including the wrongs and injustices you've perpetrated against yourself.

Stop assuming unnecessary guilt. Whenever you start to say, "It's all my fault," ask yourself if your guilt is real or imagined. Have you sinned or are you wrongly accusing yourself? I went through a terrible siege of guilt after my husband, George, died; not because I hadn't been a good wife or because there were bad feelings unsettled between us but because I was convinced I should have known he was going to have a heart attack. He had two in 1976 before he had open heart surgery, and I'd been positive since then that I'd be able to spot the signs far in advance of any attack. Looking back, I could see that they were there but neither he nor I had identified them as such. He was terribly tired, but he'd been working hard on a new project at work. His shoulders and arms were aching, but he had bursitis and had been playing basketball with Brian, so I attributed his discomfort to that. He had a slight case of indigestion, but nothing out of the ordinary. But, for a period of several weeks, I was certain it was all my fault he'd died, because I hadn't spotted those symptoms.

I phoned his doctor, who assured me that there had been no obvious signals. I knew, intellectually, that George had had two heart attacks previously and that if anyone could have spotted signs, he could have. But he didn't suspect anything, either. And, I reasoned, if *he* didn't know, how could I? Still, I couldn't shake the guilt until I got a note from a friend in Kansas. She referred to one of my favorite Scriptures, Psalms 139:16: "... In Thy book they were all written, The days that were ordained for me, When as yet there was not one of them."

The only way I was able to get beyond the imagined guilt that was haunting me was by turning to and trusting in God's Word. For days, every time I would assume that unnecessary guilt, I would quote that verse aloud and remind myself that ultimately George's life had been in God's hands, not in mine.

Whether your guilt is legitimate or not, don't take it on yourself. No one is capable of bearing such a heavy burden. Hand it over to God. Accept His grace. Reject the lie that anything can be *all* your fault.

Learn to differentiate between sin and error. An error is a mistake; sin is direct disobedience and defiance of God's will.

The guilt you experience when you sin is legitimate; the guilt you think you should feel when you blunder or make an honest mistake is not. Sin must be confessed and forsaken, but when you make a mistake, you should do whatever you can to correct it, then drop the matter and move on. I've never forgotten what my child psychology professor once said: "The errors you make may make you feel uncomfortable, and that's good because you learn from them, but they shouldn't make you feel guilty. After all, what you do probably won't change the course of history."

Lie Number Four: "I'm Worthless"

We've talked about this fourth lie before, but since it's probably the most prevalent of them all, I want to mention it again. It is, *"I'm worthless."* This attitude historically seems to be more predominant among women than men, although women today are more aware than ever before that they do have worth. The December, 1984, issue, *Glamour* magazine reported that the percentage of women who agreed with the statement, "I am an important person," was up to 66 percent in 1980 from only 11 percent in 1940.

The assumption that she is worthless affects all areas of a woman's life. Statistics show that women who are physically abused by their husbands think they are only getting what they deserve, so they stay and are continually brutalized rather than trying to get help.

Carol drove off her husband because she couldn't believe a man who was as handsome and sought after as he would actually want her for a wife. Consequently, she mistrusted him and was constantly accusing him of flirting with other women and kept predicting he'd leave her for another woman. One day he finally left, but not because of another woman. He told me he was brokenhearted but that there was no way he could contend with Carol's insecurities.

Linda turned down a lucrative promotion, which she richly deserved, because she was convinced she didn't deserve such good fortune. She still believed the lie that she'd been told as a child by an aunt with whom she lived, that she'd never amount to anything when she grew up. So Linda stifled her career, because in her company, as in most, when an employee rejected a promotion, he or she wasn't asked again.

Overcoming Feelings of Worthlessness

If you believe you are worthless, you are lying to yourself. The truth is: *You are not worthless!* You are of infinite value to God. Dennis T. DeHaan has noted: "Our heavenly Father loves us for who we are. And He gives us another basis for self-worth—Jesus' death on the cross for our sins. Sin is a universal, devastating aftereffect of Adam's fall, and we all are trapped by it. God broke down that barrier by affirming our special worth through sending His Son into the world to pay sin's penalty for you and for me."

Another truth is: *You are worth something to yourself and others.* Everyone goes through times when she thinks she doesn't matter much, but that isn't true. Even when your mate seems to tune you out or your friends don't call or your children act like they don't know the meaning of *respect,* you still matter to them. Nathaniel Hawthorne observed, "Every individual has a place to fill in the world and is important in some respect, whether he chooses to be so or not."

The secret to overcoming feelings of worthlessness is to find that special place God has designed for you to fill, then to contribute as much as you can in as many ways as you can, and to make it your goal to "grow in the grace and knowledge of our Lord and Savior Jesus Christ . . ." (2 Peter 3:18).

Lie Number Five: "I Have to Be Perfect"

A fifth lie you might tell yourself is, "I have to be perfect." This detracts immensely from feelings of self-worth because no one is perfect, and if you think you should be, you will never measure up to your unrealistic expectations or think you're good enough. Dr. David D. Burns, who has studied the effects of perfectionism, wrote, "... evidence suggests that compulsive perfectionism is not only unhealthful, producing mood disorders such as depression, anxiety and stress, but also self-defeating in terms of productivity, personal relationships and self-esteem" (*Reader's Digest*, March, 1985).

Perfectionism makes you feel inadequate because it is impossible to attain, and this distorts your self-image. Perfectionism makes you feel incompetent because it stops you from trying. This stifles creativity, thwarts accomplishment, and keeps you from becoming all God meant you to be. This lessens your self-esteem. Dr. Burns also observed, "There is, after all, a payoff in trying to be perfect; it protects you from risking criticism, failure or disapproval. But it robs you of growth, adventure and the opportunity to live life to the fullest."

Overcoming Perfectionism

If you've been telling yourself that you have to be perfect, you've been lying to yourself. There are several things you can do to start deprogramming that lie. Begin by *being realistic about yourself and your limitations as God is*. Scripture assures us that God doesn't expect perfection from us, just honest effort and obedience. "He has not dealt with us according to our sins, Nor rewarded us according to our iniquities ... For He Himself knows our frame; He is mindful that we are but dust" (Psalms 103:10, 14). You need to remember, as God does, that you're only human.

Understand God's definition of perfect. Our definition of perfect doesn't match His. *The New Britannica-Webster Dictionary* defines perfect as "being entirely without fault or defects; satisfying all requirements." Unfortunately, that's usually how we define perfect, too. No wonder we have difficulty liking ourselves. None of us is entirely without faults or defects.

Fortunately, that is not God's definition of perfect. In Scripture, the word we translate as *perfect* usually means "complete or finished, having no lacks." From God's perspective, each of us is created exactly as He wants us to be, despite what we label "defects" or "imperfections." He does not see them as such. To Him, every single person He created is "perfect," complete and finished, having no lacks.

Do what you can. Perfectionists believe they should be able to do everything and do it perfectly. That's not what God requires of us. Jesus clarified what God expects from us, and what we should expect from ourselves, when Mary anointed Him at the home of Simon the leper. The men who were present, including the self-righteous Judas Iscariot, castigated her for wasting the expensive spikenard ointment on such a lavish gesture. They accused her: ". . . this perfume might have been sold for over three hundred denarii, and the money given to the poor . . ." (Mark 14:5).

I can imagine how she must have felt. In her place, I'd have been embarrassed, thinking I'd made a fool of myself, and angry because those men had judged me unfairly and misinterpreted my motive. But Jesus intervened and defended her. He said, "Let her alone; why do you bother her? . . . She has done what she could . . ." (Mark 14:6, 8). His words illustrate that all God expects of us is that we do what we can. You don't need to try to be perfect; just to do your best.

Jesus said, "You shall know the truth, and the truth shall make you free" (John 8:32). Discovering the truth about yourself frees you to become God's special woman. Unencumbered by lies, girded in truth, you are able to move toward the goal of self-actualization, "confident of this very thing, that He who began a good work in you will perfect it until the day of Christ Jesus" (Philippians 1:6).

Workshop

The Lies You Tell Yourself

I. The following quiz will help you evaluate whether or not you are believing and acting on old lies which detract from your self-worth.

	Almost always	Usually	Sometimes	Almost never
1. I hold grudges.				
2. I blame myself when something negative happens.				
3. I think a lot about the past.				
4. I blame the past for what my life is like right now.				
5. I don't feel I have much to contribute.				
6. I assume unnecessary guilt.				
7. I am a perfectionist.				
8. I am unreasonably hard on myself when I make a mistake.				

	Almost always	Usually	Sometimes	Almost never
9. I have difficulty forgiving myself.				
10. I feel inadequate and incompetent.				
11. I dwell on what I can't do rather than on what I might possibly accomplish.				
12. I feel I am at fault when something goes wrong.				
13. I am threatened by change.				
14. I'm afraid I can never change.				

Now tally your score. Give yourself 4 points for each "almost always" response; 3 for each "usually"; 2 for each "sometimes"; and 1 for every "almost never."

If your score falls in the 46–56 range, you have not accepted the truth that you are no longer the person you once were. In many ways you are denying your new creation. You need to identify and eliminate the old lies that are destroying your self-worth.

If your score was in the 32–45 range, overall your self-concept is being negatively affected by the old lies. In many ways, you still see yourself as you were but, although it is a struggle, you are starting to believe that you are no longer the same person you once were. You need to work at seeking the truth.

If your score was in the 18–31 point range, your view of yourself is quite healthy. You recognize that you have some problems with your self-worth and that there's room for improvement, but you also accept and appreciate yourself in healthy ways. You acknowledge positive truths about yourself.

If your score was 14–18, you're almost too good to be true. Are you certain you were honest with yourself? Remember, nobody's perfect!

II. This exercise will help you identify some of the lies you may be telling yourself. In the spaces below, write one lie you have been telling yourself in each area; then write a sentence explaining why it isn't true. Be very specific.

   1. A lie you have been telling yourself about overcoming the past. _____
   _____

   2. A lie you have been telling yourself about guilt.
   _____
   _____

   3. A lie you have been telling yourself about your worth. _____
   _____

   4. A lie you have been telling yourself about being perfect. _____
   _____

   5. A lie you have been telling yourself about changing. _____
   _____

Part II

Improving Your Self-Image

Chapter Four

———— ·❦· ————

Learning to Love
Yourself

Now that you have a better understanding about what self-worth is and how it develops and are aware of some of the problems you might confront during the process of becoming God's special woman, it's time to take that first, crucial step toward self-actualization by improving your self-image. You need to develop a plan of action so you can appraise yourself realistically and learn to appreciate what you see when you look at yourself.

When I was in college, I set aside an entire weekend to study for a difficult test in a horrendous, six-unit class—Western Civilization. Every student had to take that course; it was a graduation requirement, regardless of major. So, I promised myself that weekend that there'd be no dates, no phone calls, no running out to the student union for coffee. As usual, the sorority house was almost deserted on Saturday night. I was laboriously memorizing the major factors which contributed to the start of the industrial revolution when I heard a blood-curdling scream and glass breaking. I ran out of my room and down the hallway toward the sound of sobs and shattering glass. When I realized it was coming from Betsy's room, I threw open the door and ran in, not knowing what I might find.

There was Betsy, sitting on the foot of her bed, crying, and the mirror over her dresser was broken to bits. It appeared she'd thrown a shoe at it then used the heel to pulverize the broken glass. I ran over to the bed, hugged her, and asked what had happened. "I hate myself," she sobbed. "I'm so stupid and ugly. I don't want to look at myself ever again!"

After a bit of prodding, with time out to calm a very upset housemother, I found out that Betsy's boyfriend had a date with another girl that night, one Betsy was convinced was prettier and smarter and wittier and a better dancer.

Breaking the mirror may have made Betsy feel better for the moment, but it did not solve her problem. It didn't alter who she was or how she looked or change her in any way.

Many women react the same way Betsy did when they look into the mirror of self. They don't like what they see so they "break" the mirror and stop looking at themselves, and hope that by destroying the reflection they have solved their self-image problems. But, like Betsy, ignoring what they see doesn't make those problems go away or change them in any way. When you look into the mirror of self, if you don't like what you see, there are two things you can do: stop looking or change what you see. Destroying the mirror will not improve your self-image. To do that, you have to change what it reflects.

What Is This Thing Called Self-Love?

I'm going to suggest several things you can do that can improve the reflection you see when you look into the mirror of self. They are all predicated on one simple concept: *If you are going to improve your self-image, you must learn to love yourself.*

Love is one of the most powerful forces in the world. The apostle Paul ranked it first of the three most important, enduring Christian qualities. He said, "Now abide faith, hope, love, these three; but the greatest of these is love" (1 Corinthians 13:13).

Love is powerful because it motivates your thoughts and actions. When you love people, you care about what happens to them. You are sensitive to their feelings and needs. You want to help and serve them and see good things happen to them. When you love yourself, you care enough to want the best for yourself. You treat yourself kindly and fairly.

Love is powerful because it affects your relationships with others in positive ways. It helps you reach out to others. Someone observed, "A person who respects and values himself is much more likely to be able to do the same for others. When we are not sure who we are, we are uneasy. We try to find out what the other person would like us to say before we speak, would like us to do before we act. When we are insecure, our relationship to others is governed not by what they need but by our needs. Authentic people ... are *there*, not only for themselves but for others. No energies are wasted in protecting a shaky ego."

In his book, *Mere Morality* (Eerdmans, 1983, p. 51). Lewis B. Smedes notes that "self-love can be a means of loving others. You cannot love anyone effectively if you hate yourself ... We must not squander the energy we need to care for others by failing to take care of ourselves ... You love yourself as a means of loving others."

As I teach and counsel, I am amazed at how many women truly dislike themselves. They are overly critical of themselves, never give themselves the benefit of a doubt, and do not enjoy life. Dr. Archibald Hart stresses: "The development of realistic self-knowledge in a person with low self-esteem invariably requires that many distortions be corrected. It is common to find persons whose image of themselves comes from an earlier part of their lives and bears no relation to who they are now" (*Feeling Free*, Revell, 1978, p. 127).

Yvonne is an example of such a woman. She is a lovely, soft-spoken, tall, thin, willowy young woman, who always sold herself short and settled for second best because she saw herself as a misfit. Consequently, she always dated men who treated her shabbily and chose friends who were superficial, and who had little class and no sensitivity. At work, although she is extremely talented and intelligent, she never exerted herself, so was passed over for promotions and treated disrespectfully by her supervisors. Everyone in the office always dumped the "dirty" work on her.

Yvonne's problem was that she did not love herself. When she looked into the mirror of self, she saw a gangly, uncoordinated thirteen-year-old ugly duckling of a girl (who had long since transformed into a swan) who grew too tall too fast and looked like an Amazon next to her junior-high-school classmates; a girl who, to keep from being embarrassed, withdrew and became painfully shy. So, when it came to friends and a social life, she took what was available instead of seeking out the best for herself. Sadly, although she grew into a beautiful woman, with a model's figure and sweet personality, she still saw herself as that young girl she detested for so many years.

Yvonne's story has a happy ending. When I visited with her the other evening, she was bubbly, happy, and self-assured. Although she recently received a much deserved promotion, she is job hunting because she's decided there's not enough chance for advancement in her present position. I was amazed at the change in her. When I asked what had caused it, she thought for a moment, then said, "Well, for one thing I started looking at all the people around me and I realized that they aren't any nicer than I am and most of them can't do the job as well as I can. I realized I'm not so bad after all. But mainly I just got tired of having a lousy self-image, so I decided to look at myself differently. *I decided if I don't respect and love myself, no one else will either."*

Yvonne is a different person—actually, she is well on her way to becoming God's special woman—because of that decision. Obviously, wanting to love yourself and doing it are two different things. Victor Hugo observed, "The supreme happiness in life is the conviction that we are loved . . . loved for ourselves or in spite of ourselves." Developing self-worth God's way frees us to love ourselves because of what we are rather than in spite of it.

Be Good to Yourself

Let's look at some things you can do to learn to love yourself. One is, *be good to yourself.* The other day when I was driving, a billboard caught my eye. There was a huge red heart, the universal symbol for love, followed by the word YOURSELF. Under that, the sentence, DON'T SMOKE! That message reminded me that we all need signs in our lives to remind us to love and be good to ourselves.

Have you ever thought about how you treat yourself? Most of us do not. We think about how we treat others or how others treat us, but not about the way we treat ourselves. Many people treat themselves badly. They say unkind things about themselves, judge themselves unfairly, are supercritical of themselves, and feel guilty if they do something nice for themselves. In his book, *Peace of Mind* (Simon and Schuster), Joshua L. Liebman noted that "Many people go through life committing partial suicide—destroying their talents, energies, creative qualities. To learn how to be good to oneself is often more difficult than to learn how to be good to others."

I think the reason for that is because we operate on the false assumption that being good to yourself is selfish. Yet, Scripture clearly indicates that God wants you to be good to yourself. In 1 Corinthians 6:19, 20 Paul exhorts Christians to take care of their bodies: "Do you not know that your body is a temple of the Holy Spirit who is in you, whom you have from God, and that you are not your own? For you have been bought with a price: therefore, glorify God in your body."

In Philippians 4:8 he encourages us to be good to our minds by letting our thoughts dwell on whatever is true, honorable, right, pure, lovely, of good repute, excellent, and worthy of praise. That certainly implies you shouldn't cloud your thoughts and emotions with unwarranted bad images of yourself or treat yourself disrespectfully.

I've been learning a lot about being good to myself since George died. George was very good to me. He spoiled and pampered me. He complimented me for little everyday things I did that often are taken for granted, like making a superlative batch of homemade chicken-noodle soup or sewing on a loose button. He also bragged to me and others about what a good writer I am. And, he'd remind me if I was overextending myself or getting too tired or spending too many hours at my desk or not exercising enough.

Now that he's gone, there's no one to do those things for me—except myself. One of the first things I learned in my widow's support group was that I have to learn how to be good to myself, because my well-being and that of those I love depends on how well I treat myself. I've also learned that being good to myself isn't being selfish or self-centered. It doesn't mean you don't reach out to others but that you respond in positive ways to yourself.

I don't know what you need to do to be good to yourself. To stimulate your imagination, let me share some things that I, and other women, have done. Linda, who loves to write letters, ordered stationery embossed with her initials. Connie, who is tied to a desk during the day, decided to treat herself to a massage and facial once a month. Mary stopped doing housework in the afternoon while her three-year-old twins nap and started reading and relaxing during that time. Irene, who dislikes talking on the phone, bought an inexpensive answering machine, so she can control who she talks to and when. You'll notice that most of this "personalized pampering" is simply being thoughtful and considerate of oneself in little ways.

I've done myself a lot of little favors in these past months since George died. I get my nails manicured regularly, something I never wanted to take the time to do before. I've set aside time to read, something that had gotten lost in the hustle and bustle of everyday life. I planted a lot of roses in the front yard, because roses lift my spirits. I love the sight and smell of them. I bought a rolltop desk for my bedroom, something I've always wanted but didn't have a place for. I love sitting at it and writing when I can't sleep. Once a week I spend quality time with a friend I haven't seen for a while. These are all little things but they are the fiber and fabric of life. They make me feel better about myself.

Practice the Golden Rule

Perhaps you need to practice the Golden Rule in a new way. Along with doing unto others as you would have them do unto you, you need to treat yourself the way you wish others would treat you. For example, I want others to be kind to me, so I should be kind to myself. I want them to understand me, think and speak well of me, and forgive me, so I should be understanding of myself, be willing to forgive myself, and to think and speak well of myself. People respect and admire people who respect themselves and the Lord. If you have a tendency not to apply the Golden Rule to yourself, ask yourself, would I do this to someone else? Would I say this about her? Would I condemn her for this? If not, then don't treat yourself that way either.

Take Care of Yourself

Part of being good to yourself involves *taking care of yourself* physically and emotionally. Most of you are so accustomed to taking care of others or having others take care of you that you probably forget to take care of yourselves. In fact, many women feel guilty when they take time or spend money to stay healthy or improve themselves. Money you spend on keeping your body and mind in shape is well spent. Time you devote to maintaining your personal appearance and developing your skills and talents is as necessary to your survival as food and water.

I believe there are two rules you have to follow if you are going to take care of yourself properly. The first is, don't get "too" of anything—too tired, too upset, too emotionally involved, too busy, too concerned, too hungry, too wrapped up in yourself, too involved in too many things—because when you do, you end up neglecting yourself.

Scripture teaches that moderation and self-control are virtues. Being "too" of anything is detrimental to well-being and self-image. For example, when I get too tired, I don't do as good a job, so I feel inadequate. When I'm too upset or too emotionally involved, I don't think or reason well, so I make mistakes or errors in judgment, which make me feel incompetent or foolish. When I get too wrapped up in myself, I usually get a king-sized case of self-pity. Extremes are definitely image detractors.

The second rule for caring for yourself is input good things, because what goes into your body and mind affects how you feel about yourself, your life, and your relationships. Listen to good music, engage in good conversation, read good literature, think good thoughts, eat good food (not just food that tastes good but is good for you), keep good company. Practice being good to yourself. Think something positive about yourself and do something nice for yourself every day. It will improve your self-image.

Improve the External

Another necessity for loving yourself and enhancing self-image is to *improve the external.* It's a proven fact that human beings are sensitive to their environment. You are affected by it and respond to it. Surroundings, from cloudy skies to the color of wallpaper on the family-room wall, affect your moods and behavior.

There is one part of your environment you carry with you wherever you go—your body. The body is the environment which houses the soul. The way it looks and performs affects how you feel about yourself. And, the way you dress, speak, and behave reflects those feelings and affects how others approach and respond to you. Therefore, making positive changes in your personal appearance can improve your self-image. There's no doubt that looking good makes you feel better about yourself.

I'm always fascinated by the "makeover" articles and ads in women's magazines, where beauty experts transform ordinary-looking women into extraordinary beauties, with the help of makeup and a new hairstyle. Most of us are so accustomed to the way we look, we don't think about possibilities for improvement. We look in the mirror and say, "Ho hum. That's me." Yet almost every woman could benefit from some kind of external "makeover," if not for beauty's sake, simply to give herself a lift. Something as simple as using a different shade of lipstick or nail polish can be a great esteem booster.

There's something each one of you could do to improve

your appearance. Perhaps you need to work on your figure. Eating properly takes off pounds; exercising whittles off inches. Perhaps you need to change your hairstyle. Your hairstyle should match your life-style and your personality. For example, if you are a busy, on-the-go person, you need an easy-to-care-for hairstyle that doesn't require much maintenance. If you are a casual, laid-back person, a severe, sophisticated hairstyle won't reflect the real you and you probably won't be comfortable with it. Changing your hairstyle is an easy, inexpensive way to lift your spirits or change your image. If you've always had short hair, letting it grow will give you more versatility in how you wear your hair and an opportunity to experiment with various styles. and, if you don't like it, you can always cut it. If you've been wearing your hair long, trying a shorter style may give you a whole new outlook about yourself. And, if you don't like it, you can always let it grow.

Revamp Your Makeup

Perhaps you need to revamp your makeup. When I was young, we wore makeup to match the color of our clothes. When I wore a bright red blouse, I wore bright red lipstick. When I wore a pink sweater, I switched to pink lipstick. I know now that makeup should be geared to your skin tone, not your clothing.

For years I used an orange-toned foundation, powder, and blush because I wear so much red. I never understood why I couldn't get a soft glowing look until a clerk where I buy my cosmetics suggested that, for my skin coloring, I needed a pink-toned makeup. My first reaction was, "What! Wear pink blusher when I'm wearing a red sweater?" But I tried her suggestion and was astounded at the difference that one simple change made.

If you want to run a check on your makeup, there are

dozens of books on the market by experts who are more than willing to tell you what you need to do to become a more beautiful you. Two of my favorites are *Dress With Style* by Joanne Wallace (Revell, 1983) and *Alive with Color* by my friend Leatrice Eiseman (Acropolis, 1983). Although they use different approaches for analyzing color, both tell how to improve self-image by enhancing your inner and outer selves. Or you can consult the salesclerk in the cosmetics department of your local department store. Most of them are trained by manufacturers to act as beauty consultants to their customers. And, many beauty salons employ makeup artists, as well as hairdressers and manicurists.

Revamp Your Wardrobe

Perhaps you need to revamp your wardrobe. Sometimes we get locked into one way of thinking about ourselves and that is reflected in the style and color of clothing we wear. I know a beautiful young woman who, when she was in her twenties, dressed like she was fifty. She wore very conservative styles and drab colors. Many of her blouses, dresses, and jackets were a dull, green-toned yellow or gray, two of the worst possible colors she could have chosen for her skin tone and the color of her hair and eyes. She always looked washed out and older than she was.

This was before color analysis became popular, but I convinced her that she needed to add a little sparkle and some new, younger looking styles to her wardrobe. Believe it or not, she had never shopped for a wardrobe. She'd just always bought something when she needed it or if she saw something she liked when she was walking through a store. So, for a year, I went shopping with her every season, to teach her how to select a coordinated wardrobe. Once she started trying on clothes, she realized that blues, pinks, lavenders, and reds with blue in them were her colors. We salvaged a lot of the gray in her closet by adding colorful accessories—belts, earrings, necklaces, scarves. But, we decided the icky yellows had to go.

Revamping her wardrobe completely changed that young woman's image. She became less reserved and more relaxed, and gained self-confidence, all because of the way she dressed.

You don't have to spend a lot of money to build a good wardrobe. You need to buy clothes that mix and match. It's also fun to have one or two items that are "out of character" for you. I'm basically a tailored, sweater-and-suit-type person, but I have one slinky, black satin evening outfit that I love wearing because I feel like an entirely different person when I put it on.

Because you are so sensitive to this environment called the body, it's important never to let yourself go. Even if you're going to be stuck in the house all day with the kids, comb your hair, and put on a dab of makeup. Even if you scrub floors and toilets, wash a lot of dishes, and do your own gardening, like most women do, take care of your nails. Wear gloves and keep your nails manicured. They don't have to be long and gaudy. Short nails, neatly trimmed, with a coat of clear polish, look attractive. How you look, even when you are alone, can affect your disposition. There's no doubt that taking care *of* yourself can make you care more *for* yourself. Improving externals does improve self-image.

Be Yourself

Another tactic for learning to love yourself and improve self-image is, *be yourself.* Don't try to be something you're not or try to imitate someone else. You will, of course, use bits and pieces of others as role models, but God didn't intend for you to be anybody but yourself. Instead of trying to copy someone else, you need to accept and appreciate your uniqueness. Each of you has something special to contribute that is exclusively yours. If you are uniquely created, you must have something valuable and different to share. Bruce Barton, well-known Christian teacher and writer, believes "we have missed the full impact of the Gospel if we have not discovered what it is to be ourselves, loved by God, irreplaceable in His sight, unique among our fellow men ... If you have anything valuable to contribute to the world, it will come through the expression of your own personality—that single spark of divinity that sets you off and makes you different from every other living creature" (*Reader's Digest*, "Points to Ponder," June, 1981).

Trying to be something you aren't traps you into comparing yourself with others, which creates envy and jealousy, along with feelings of inadequacy and dissatisfaction with yourself. You want to be what someone else is instead of being yourself and get to the point where nothing you do is good enough because you imagine you don't measure up, by comparison, and your self-image is severely berated.

The secret of being yourself isn't to compare yourself to others but to compare what you are now to what you can be. Syndicated columnist Sydney J. Harris noted, "However diverse their talents, temperaments and differences, all great achievers have one trait in common: They never bother to compare themselves with others, but are content to run their own race on their own terms."

God never asks you to be something you aren't; only to choose to be yourself. Every one of you can be the best at something. My friend's mentally retarded son makes the best blueberry muffins in the world. My dad, who had a fourth-grade education and no formal training, could repair absolutely anything, from a broken china cup to an automobile engine. My son's trumpet teacher, a soft-spoken, easygoing man, has an uncanny ability to motivate his teenage students to practice their lessons.

You lose your way, your purpose and meaning in life when you try to follow in someone else's footsteps or live up to his or her expectations. Eventually, you'll lose sight of who you are and risk ending up thinking of yourself as a nobody. In his newspaper column, Sydney J. Smith advised, "Whatever you are by nature, keep to it; never desert your line of talent. *Be what nature intended you for, and you will succeed; be anything else, and you will be ten thousand times worse than nothing.*"

Don't Expect Too Much of Yourself

But, you also need to have realistic expectations. *Don't expect too much of yourself.* Set limits. Don't try to be a superwoman or spread yourself too thin. Overload results in incompetence and eventual failure, which makes you feel lousy about yourself. When you try to do too much, you can't do anything well. When you try to do something for which you aren't trained or don't have ability, you're programming yourself for failure and undermining your self-esteem. Too often, we pridefully impose unrealistic expectations on ourselves.

The other day I was watching a television interview with a well-known character actor. The talk-show host asked him if he ever regretted being tagged a character actor, rather than a star. He laughed and said, "All of my life I've had the privilege of working at my craft while a lot of stars sat home waiting for calls from their agents. I'm always busy because life needs a lot more supporting players than it does stars." He is a wise man. He doesn't expect or want to be a star—just to make the most of his potential.

Henry Ward Beecher gave this sage advice about realistic expectations: "Do not be troubled because you do not have great virtue. God made a million spears of grass where He made one tree. The earth is fringed and carpeted not only with forests, but with grasses. Only have enough of little virtues and common fidelities, and you need not mourn because you are neither a hero nor a saint."

Affirm Yourself

If you want to improve your self-image, you must be yourself. You must also learn to *affirm yourself.* Affirmation is confirming that a fact is true, then applying it in a constructive way. Self-affirmation isn't tooting your own horn so loudly that you drown out others but accepting that you can play the tune and admitting that you can do it well.

Most people are much better at criticizing themselves than they are complimenting themselves. You do, of course, need to criticize yourself constructively, but when you do, you should expect to unearth positives as well as negatives. Instead, many women practice what Dr. David D. Burns calls the "binocular trick." They magnify their weaknesses and minimize their strengths. "You are either blowing things up, or shrinking them, out of proportion. You look at your imperfections through binoculars and magnify them; you look through the other end of the binoculars and shrink your good points" (*Feeling Good: The New Mood Therapy*, William Morrow, 1980).

We have problems affirming ourselves for three reasons. One, we concentrate on negatives; two, we misinterpret our findings; three, we do not know how to compliment ourselves. All of you are a mixture of faults and virtues, of shortcomings and merits. If you are going to love yourself, you must learn to concentrate on and accentuate the positives rather than dwelling on and accenting the negatives. You need to make the most of your strengths and minimize your weaknesses. You are what you perceive yourself to be, so if you eye yourself with negativity, you bring out the worst in yourself and strengthen your flaws. But, if you look at yourself from a positive perspective, inadequacies will diminish and you will start to see yourself as a capable, productive woman.

Many times women sabotage their self-esteem by concentrating on their shortcomings. For example, I am not good at math. I have no "number sense." Therefore, I would not be a good engineer, scientist, bookkeeper or accountant. And, I have absolutely no artistic ability when it comes to drawing or painting, so I could never be a fashion designer or an artist. If I concentrated on those weaknesses instead of capitalizing on my ability as a writer, I'd undermine my confidence, my career, my self-worth, and lose a large part of my identity. Instead of dwelling on those lacks, I try to make the most of the capabilities I do have.

We Misinterpret the Findings

Another reason we have difficulty affirming ourselves is that when we critique ourselves, we frequently misinterpret the findings. Sometimes we confuse strengths with weaknesses. For example, Sally is one of the most tenacious women I have ever known. She perseveres long after anyone else would have given up in despair. She refuses to quit until a job is finished and is a very principled person who will not compromise her beliefs or standards when she thinks something is right. She is also a loyal friend and has great leadership ability. All of these are positive qualities which show strength of character.

But for years, Sally didn't see them as such. When she was a child, she was stubborn, willful, and quite spoiled (the youngest of five children and the only girl). Consequently, she demanded her own way and usually got it. Everyone found it difficult to deny the curly-headed imp anything.

As Sally grew and matured in her faith, Christ tempered her selfish attitude and mellowed the negative of stubbornness into the positive of determination and molded her willfulness into tenacity. Yet, for years, Sally didn't accept herself because she misinterpreted the findings. Despite the fact that she had changed, she saw herself as the spoiled, selfish child she had been; not as the principled woman she had become. Gradually, as people admired and responded to her tenacity and competency in positive ways, she realized she had changed and that those supposed weaknesses had turned into strengths.

Many negatives or weaknesses have the seed of positive possibilities embedded within them. Sometimes a minor change in attitude or approach can turn a weakness into a strength. Wishful thinking can be channeled into optimism and creativity; arrogance into self-confidence; a need to control into an ability to lead and organize; bluntness into truthfulness; stubbornness into perseverance. Someone who is manipulative or demanding can, with effort, learn to motivate others in positive ways. Someone with a suspicious nature can be transformed into a person who is healthfully cautious yet accepting. You need to be careful not to confuse weaknesses with strengths.

Learn to Compliment Yourself

The third reason we have trouble affirming ourselves is that we do not know how to compliment ourselves, but we are masters at berating ourselves. Because we do not know how to identify or appreciate nice things about ourselves, we depend exclusively on others to do all of the positive reinforcing, and when they don't respond, our self-worth diminishes. Have you ever thought about how many negative comments you make to yourself, about yourself (most of which are expressed in silent thoughts rather than spoken words)? Compare that to how often you say something nice to yourself about yourself.

I've thought a lot about why we're so reticent to give ourselves a pat on the back for a job well done, and I've decided it's because we believe that acknowledging our accomplishments and worth is prideful. That's not true, any more than loving ourselves is egotistical. Bragging or thinking you are better than others or doing things to draw attention to yourself or putting people down to build up yourself *is* prideful, but honestly complimenting yourself is not.

When I was teaching a class about how mothers can define and meet the needs of their children, someone asked if I thought the quality of time mothers spend with their children is more important than the quantity. Before I could reply, a young woman raised her hand and said, "I'd like to answer that, if I may. I'm a good mother, and I've struggled with that question and come up with what I think is a satisfactory balance." I was delighted at how refreshing it was to hear that young mother affirm her worth in such an unassuming, positive way.

In her book, *Don't Shoot the Dog* (Simon and Schuster, 1984) Karen Pryor has this to say about self-affirmation: "You can deliberately use positive reinforcement on yourself. I once met a Wall Street lawyer who is an avid squash player and shouts to himself 'Way to go, Pete, atta boy!' for every good shot. He says it has improved his game tremendously since the days when he cursed himself for his errors all the time.

"But reinforcing ourselves is something we often neglect. Either it doesn't occur to us, or we demand too much of ourselves. As a result, we often go for days without letup, moving from task to task, unthanked by ourselves."

Cultivate Healthy, Constructive Relationships

You do need to affirm yourself. Self-affirmation is a vital part of improving self-image. So is *cultivating healthy, constructive relationships*. If you're going to learn how to love yourself, you need to associate with people who care for you and will affirm your worth, who love you enough to build you up, help you face reality, and encourage you to grow in grace and knowledge of the Lord. Instead, many times women lock into relationships that tear them down. It's as if they are trying to affirm their lack of worth so seek out people who will validate their low, and usually erroneous, opinion of themselves.

In most instances, the inability to cultivate healthy, constructive relationships can be traced back to childhood. Girls who were berated by their families, especially by their fathers, date men who belittle them. Women who were abused or demeaned when they were young, marry men who continue that pattern. Daughters who have mothers who constantly criticized them and emphasized only their faults, who refused to compliment or praise them for their efforts and accomplishments, tend to do the same thing to themselves and their children, and usually keep going back to their mothers for negative reinforcement, even though such relationships debilitate them.

One of my friends, I'll call her Ann, who is in her mid-fifties, is still so severely affected by her encounters with her seventy-six-year-old mother that she cries for days after she spends time with her. Her mother is able to reduce this otherwise happy, self-assured, successful woman to an emotional heap of rubble in minutes.

Recently Ann's husband insisted she stop seeing her mother, who is quite wealthy and lives in a retirement community. He was tired of seeing his wife hurt and having their home life disrupted. Ann was torn. Even though theirs is a destructive relationship, she has felt obligated to continue it because she is a Christian and it *is* her mother.

She was so confused she went to her pastor for counsel. I was pleased when he advised her to comply with her husband's wishes. He told her that her husband had her best interests at heart, but that her mother obviously did not. He assured her that her mother was the one who was responsible for causing the breach in the relationship and that there was nothing else she could do. After much prayer, Ann reached a compromise in her thinking. She was convinced she wouldn't be a bad Christian if she told her mother she would not spend time with her until she was willing to treat her with respect.

Ann is like a different person since she relinquished the burden of that relationship. She didn't break off all contact. She sends her mother cards and gifts, and talks to her on the phone sometimes, but the minute she starts getting on Ann's case, Ann hangs up. She no longer has to live with the image of herself as a bad daughter.

Healthy, constructive relationships are a must for improving self-image, but it isn't always possible to get out of every relationship that tears you down. If a woman is married to a man who demeans her or doesn't show appreciation, or has children who are disrespectful of her and her wishes, she can't just walk away. Instead, she has to learn to compensate by refusing to internalize their opinions. She must evaluate the truth in every charge or criticism and discard whatever is not valid. She can choose not to let uncaring individuals diminish her opinion of herself. She can compensate by eliminating many negative aspects of a relationship and can eliminate some destructive relationships altogether. No one needs so-called friends who are unkind to them, who are jealous of them, who undermine their feelings of worth, or who use them. Nothing makes a person feel more worthless or foolish than being used.

For example, Janice and Emily were friends for years. Janice is a sweet, tenderhearted woman while Emily tends to be caustic and overbearing, but according to Janice, Emily has a heart of gold and would do anything for anyone. In the course of a few months two positive things had happened to Janice: she redecorated her house and she got a promotion. Her house, which she did without the help of a decorator, looks absolutely fabulous and her new position has given her a chance to travel, conduct workshops, and come in contact with some new, exciting, important people.

Instead of sharing her friend's happiness and success, Emily has become hypercritical of everything Janice says or does, to the point where she is undermining Janice's self-confidence. When Janice dropped by to see me, she was in tears because Emily had told her what a horrible job she'd done choosing the sofa and chairs for the living room. According to Emily, the colors and size of the furniture were all wrong. And, she spent half an hour belittling Janice's business colleagues and her promotion by elaborating on what was wrong with the way she was approaching her new job. She also accused her of neglecting her husband, Stan, who is more than pleased with both the house and his wife's career.

"Why is she doing this to me, Jo? I just don't understand why she keeps attacking me like this," Janice choked through tears.

When I shared my opinion that Emily is jealous and threatened by Janice's success, her eyes widened. "Why, that's exactly what Stan said!" she gasped.

As we talked about what she could do, I suggested the following guidelines I use when evaluating the value and necessity of a relationship.

Evaluating Relationships

Is the relationship worth saving? What purpose is it serving? Is it good for both parties? Sometimes people outgrow one another. Not all friendships are till death us do part. Some are based on a specific set of needs and circumstances and when those change, so does the relationship.

Can you still make positive contributions to each other? What do you have to offer each other? Does the person build you up or tear you down? When a relationship reaches the point where most of the input is from a negative point of view, it becomes destructive rather than constructive and may have outlived its benefits. Staying locked into debilitating relationships keeps you from becoming involved in fruitful ones where you can minister in positive, effective ways.

Can you change the structure of the relationship? Can you salvage it if you do things differently? Perhaps you don't need to do away with a relationship but approach it differently, as Ann did with her mother. Janice restructured her relationship with Emily. She stopped confiding in her about her job and saw her less frequently. She realized that in some ways she was inadvertently setting herself up for Emily's attacks. Now that they meet once in a while for lunch, they have so much to catch up on that the negative elements in their friendship are fading.

Do you want to continue the relationship? Do you *feel* like investing time and energy in the relationship? Do you like the person? (Why do we think we should be friends with people we dislike or don't enjoy being with?) Do you have mutual needs and interests? If not, you shouldn't continue the relationship, because it won't be healthy for either person.

Will you be used or be useful? Nobody should become or stay involved in a relationship that is obviously self-serving to only one of the parties. You need to learn the difference between serving others and being used by them. For example, I am friends with several younger women who think of me as a surrogate mother. I don't spend a lot of time with any of them, but we keep in touch and when one of them has a problem or needs help I'm usually the first person she calls. On the surface, it seems as if I do all of the giving and they do all of the taking, but I do not believe those young women are using me. Instead, I am useful to them and view my relationship with each as a way to fulfill my role as an "older" woman, which Paul described in Titus 2:3–5. And, I get a lot out of our association, too; surrogate daughters, sons-in-law and grandchildren, and a broad outlet for my mother-hen instinct.

Once you learn the difference between being used and being useful, you can protect yourself from unnecessary hurts and humiliation, be more effective as you minister, and improve your self-image. Remember, unhealthy, destructive relationships destroy self-worth.

Opt for Quality

Finally, if you want to learn to love yourself and improve your self-image, you must do everything within your power to *live a quality existence*. Evan Esar observed, "You can't do anything about the length of your life, but you can do something about its width and depth." A scientific theory states that like begets like. If you want to *see* a quality person when you look into the mirror of self, you have to *be* a quality person. First-rate people never settle for second-best.

When I was a teenager, I hated to sew, probably because I was so impatient. When I was in the ninth grade, I was forced to take sewing in home economics. First we made napkins, then an apron, then a simple gathered skirt. The final project was to make a dress. I vividly remember choosing a tiny, pink-and-white checkered cotton fabric and the easiest pattern I could find. The teacher made us baste each piece and submit it to her for approval before we stitched it up. Once she okayed something, I sewed it as quickly as I could. I wasn't concerned with what the underseams looked like. All I cared about was getting the thing put together and what the dress looked like on the outside.

My teacher turned the finished product back to me with a big, red "F" attached to the collar and instructions to rip out every seam and do it over. But she went a step further. She also attached a note, which I still have in my high-school yearbook. It said, "I am disappointed that you chose to do such a poor job when you are capable of doing so much better. You should be aware that the underseams affect the way a garment fits and looks. If you want to wear a pretty dress, you have to do quality workmanship."

That's a lesson I've never forgotten. (I thought about it as I tediously ripped out every stitch.) Someone once said that halfway is the same as not getting there. Mediocrity and slovenliness are image detractors. Your improvement happens in proportion to your commitment. If you do not strive for excellence or don't do all you can to make your life matter, to make every thought, movement, and deed count for eternity, you're selling yourself short. If you are going to become God's special woman and improve your self-image, you must opt for quality.

Workshop

Learning to Love Yourself

I. First, you're going to take an inventory of some qualities that make you special. Print your name in capital letters down the left column, then beside each letter write a strength of yours—a unique quality of special talent—that starts with that letter. If you have a short first name, use your middle or last name, too. For example, Jean might write that she is Joyful, Energetic, Ambitious, and Neat.

II. This quiz will help you examine how well you love yourself. Think about each question before you answer. Rate yourself on a scale of 1 to 10, 10 being the best. When you finish, tally your score.

    1. I want what is best for myself.
    2. I treat myself kindly.
    3. I am fair when I judge myself.
    4. I am willing to give myself the benefit of a doubt.
    5. I speak kindly about myself to others.
    6. I do something nice for myself every day.

7. I treat myself the way I want other people to treat me.

8. I don't get "too" of anything.

9. I listen to good music.

10. I engage in good conversation.

11. I read good literature.

12. I eat food that is good for me.

13. I think good thoughts.

14. I keep good company.

15. I think well of myself.

16. I use others as role models but try to be myself.

17. I believe I have something special to contribute that is exclusively mine.

18. I compare myself to myself, rather than comparing myself to others.

19. I make the most of my strengths.

20. I minimize my weaknesses.

21. I compliment myself.

22. I cultivate healthy, constructive relationships.

23. I opt for quality by doing all I can to improve the depth and width of my life.

24. I truly believe I am in the process of becoming God's special woman.

If your score was 200–240: Are you being egotistical or is this legitimate self-love?

If your score was 150–199: Your self-image is healthy and you have a well-balanced perspective of yourself. You're ready to start cultivating self-esteem.

If your score was 100–149: Your self-image is strong in some areas but weak in others. Read back through the list and identify areas where you need to work on improving your self-image. Decide what you need to do to raise your score in each area where you scored low.

If your score was 70–99: You have a long way to go before you can truly say you love and accept yourself. Although there are some things you admire about yourself, you lack an overall sense of self-worth and have a lot of obstacles to overcome before you see yourself as you should. You need to start believing in yourself and plan specific ways to improve your self-image.

If your score was 69 or less: You do not love yourself. You probably don't even like yourself. You see few, if any, positives when you look into the mirror of self. You may need to ask your pastor, a trusted teacher, or a counselor to help you evaluate yourself realistically and search out why you cannot or won't accept yourself.

III. Here is a list of strengths, to help you see yourself in a positive way. Read through the list. Put an * by each attribute you possess. Circle five you would like to cultivate.

loving nature	generous	adventuresome
flexible	love life!	ability to listen
ability to give	ability to	relate well to
relate well to	receive	adults
kids	sense of humor	sensitivity
open	courageous	intelligent
trusting nature	empathetic	imaginative
childlike	energetic	respect of self
respect of others	varied interests	creative
intuitive	organized	sense of beauty
spontaneous	tender	responsive
loyal	realistic	playful
inventive	curious	helpful
responsible	sympathetic	compassionate

warm	independent	self-motivated
supportive	dependable	ability to change
accept change	good friend	tenacious
readily	trustworthy	clearsighted
principled	hopeful	encouraging
straightforward	honest	ability to cope
resilient	forgiving	patient
serene		

IV. Take a few minutes to think of how you can improve your self-image by revamping some externals. Using the list below, write one thing for each category that you would like to change. Next, write a sentence describing what you will do to make that change. Then do it!

1. Figure _____

_____

2. Makeup _____

_____

3. Hairstyle _____

_____

4. Clothing _____

_____

5. Overall appearance _____

_____

Part III

———◆———

Cultivating
Self-Esteem

Chapter Five

Pursuing Peace

By now, if you're applying the principles we've discussed, you should be seeing a more positive reflection when you look into the mirror of self. Once your self-image has begun to improve you're probably ready to take the second step toward self-actualization, which is cultivating self-esteem. But remember, becoming God's special woman is a never-ending growth process. There will always be facets of your self-image that need attention. You should be careful not to neglect them when you start developing characteristics which build self-esteem.

If you recall, I defined self-esteem as the way you feel about yourself and react to who and what you are. Gloria Hope Hawley called such feelings "the language of the inner person" (*Frankly Feminine*, Standard Publishing, 1978, p. 72). Your feelings are silent indicators of the thoughts and responses that are taking place in your heart and mind. The feelings you experience when you look into the mirror of self are silent indicators of your self-worth. They are barometers of the soul that measure your self-esteem, much the way a barometer measures air pressure. Your feelings show the level of your self-esteem, whether it is high or low.

People respond to external stimuli. Whatever we hear, touch, taste, smell, and see arouses feelings. I became keenly aware of that one morning when I was walking. Southern California is at its picture-postcard best in early spring. Warm winds stave off smog, the sky is bright blue, the temperature moderate. Everything is in bloom and the foothills are alive with color as ground cover explodes into variegated shades of magenta, gold, orange, red, purple, and creamy white. I was saturated with warmth, joy, peace and the assurance of God's goodness as my senses absorbed the magnificient beauty of His creation.

We also react to what we see when we look at ourselves. In his book, *Feeling Free*, Dr. Archibald Hart noted that, "As human beings we have the ability to engage in self-reflection, and this forms the basis of self-image. Out of our evaluation of this self-image, we develop a sense of self-esteem in which we feel either good or bad about what we see" (Revell, 1979, p. 19).

What Is Low Self-Esteem?

In his book *What Wives Wish Their Husbands Knew About Women*, (Tyndale, 1975, pp. 22, 23), Dr. James Dobson vividly describes what it means to have low self-esteem and to struggle with deep-seated feelings of inadequacy.

It is sitting alone in a house during the quiet afternoon hours, wondering why the phone doesn't ring . . . wondering why you have no "real" friends. It is longing for someone to talk to, soul to soul, but knowing there is no such person worthy of your trust. It is feeling that "they wouldn't like me if they knew the real me." It is becoming terrified when speaking to a group of your peers, and feeling like a fool when you get home. It is wondering why other people have so much more talent and ability than you do. It is feeling incredibly ugly and sexually unattractive. It is admitting you have become a failure as a wife and mother. It is disliking everything about yourself and wishing, constantly wishing, you could be someone else. It is feeling unloved and unlovable and lonely and sad. It is lying in bed after the family is asleep, pondering the vast emptiness inside and longing for unconditional love. It is intense self-pity. It is reaching up in the darkness to remove a tear from the corner of your eye. It is depression!

Low self-esteem is hating what you see when you look into the mirror of self, and being overwhelmed by bad feelings about yourself, which indicate there is a lack of good ones. Healthy self-esteem, on the other hand, "is to feel good about yourself in a realistic yet positive way. You realize you aren't perfect. You do not consider yourself better than others" (*Lord, What's Really Important?* Fritz Ridenour, Regal, 1978, pp. 70, 71). Healthy self-esteem means you are not engulfed by feelings of inadequacy but are able to acknowledge your worth without becoming prideful.

Make no mistake, self-esteem is essential to your well-being. Dr. Neil Clark Warren, dean of the Graduate School of Psychology at Fuller Theological Seminary, writes:

I have become convinced that the way we come to feel about ourselves determines to a great degree the kind of lives we live. For instance . . . an individual's attitude to-

ward himself radically influences his appraisals of others, so that in a very real sense he can love others only as he learns to love himself. And how a person feels about himself is being increasingly recognized as a vital factor in determining his behavior. A large number of studies have demonstrated that a person will tend to behave in ways which are consistent with his self-conception ("Self-Esteem: A Two-Track Approach—the Gospel and the Law," Theology, News and Notes, *December, 1978, p. 3*).

How to Cultivate Self-Esteem

Obviously, you cannot become God's special woman until you cultivate self-esteem. Let's talk about how to do that. Cultivating is an agricultural process. First, the farmer digs deep into the ground to break up clods of earth and bring fresh soil to the surface. At the same time, he plows under weeds, then fertilizes the soil before he plants a crop. To cultivate self-esteem, first we have to dig deep into our hearts and prepare them to receive a new crop of truth. So to cultivate self-esteem you need to weed out the old, negative, invalid feelings and fertilize the soil of your soul with reality, then sow the seeds of self-esteem and tend them as they grow.

Someone has said it is not enough for a gardener to love flowers, she must also hate weeds. To raise your self-esteem, you have to hate the weeds of self-doubt and inferiority badly enough to plow them under and plant a new crop of positive attitudes. You have to want to feel better about yourself. Dr. Dobson stresses that "women who feel inferior must seek ways to deal with it." You have to care enough about becoming God's special woman to spend effort and energy climbing the stairs toward self-actualization.

Cultivating Peace With God

In this section of the book, we're going to examine five qualities you need to cultivate if you're going to elevate your self-esteem. The first is *peace*. When you follow David's advice to "seek peace, and pursue it" (Psalms 34:14), you eliminate the weeds of worry, anxiety, and stress. You begin by cultivating peace with God, by living a holy, righteous life.

Positionally, you obtain peace with God when you receive Christ. Before you became a Christian you were God's enemy; totally alienated from Him: "You were dead in your trespasses and sins" (Ephesians 2:1). But, you ". . . were reconciled to God through the death of His Son . . ." (Romans 5:10). In a practical sense, you lose peace with God when you sin and you reconcile with Him when you confess your sins and repent.

Sin detracts from your feelings of self-worth; personal purity elevates self-esteem. Think for a moment about how you feel when you do something you know is wrong. I was having lunch with a friend and remarked that she was so quiet. She sighed and said, "I'm really feeling lousy about something I did. I said some really harsh and unnecessary things to Harry this morning before he left for work. Every once in a while I get upset about a lot of little things, then I take out my frustration on him. I guess I'm not a very good wife."

Harry would be the first person to tell you that my friend is a wonderful wife, but she wasn't feeling like one that day. She was imagining herself as a bad wife and reacting to what she saw. She couldn't relax and enjoy our lunch until she called her husband and apologized. Once she had dealt with her sin, she was at peace with him and started feeling better about herself. The same is true with your relationship with the Lord. You can't have peace with Him until you deal with your sin.

The Peace of God

You also need to cultivate the peace *of* God. God's peace is already there for you once you accept Christ, but you have to appropriate it. D. L. Moody wrote, "A great many people are trying to *make* peace, but that has already been done. God has not left it for us to do; all we have to do is enter into it."

Bob Mumford reminds us that "peace *with* God brings the peace *of* God. It is a peace that settles our nerves, floods our spirit, and in the midst of the uproar around us, gives us the assurance that everything is all right."

Billy Graham defined the peace *of* God as being able to sleep in the midst of a storm, like Jesus did when He fell asleep in the stern of the boat during a fierce storm. (*See* Mark 4:37–40.) Dr. Graham observes, "In Christ we are relaxed and at peace in the midst of the confusions, bewilderments and perplexities of life" (*Topical Encyclopedia of Living Quotations*, Bethany House, 1982). Once we are at peace *with* God and rest in the peace *of* God, we can be at peace with ourselves. We are able to relax not only physically but in our subconscious, and to feel good about ourselves.

How to Cultivate Peace

If your self-esteem is low because of agitation and anxiety, the following suggestions can help you cultivate the peace that is already yours in Christ.

One, you need to *accept that stress is an inevitable part of life.* Peace is not due to the absence of stress in our lives but to the ability to handle it properly. Shortly after George died my car broke down. I was very upset. I thought, *How could God let this happen to me, on top of all I've gone through these past few weeks.* All I know about automobiles is how to put gas in them and drive them. I was afraid some unscrupulous mechanic would take advantage of my ignorance and say I needed a lot of expensive repairs. I felt totally inadequate to handle the situation.

After my daughter Brenda listened to me cry and fuss and fume she said, "Well, Mom, I guess we can't expect problems to stop just because Daddy died. Cars breaking down are a normal part of life." Her counsel helped me immensely. Now when something goes wrong, I try to look at it as just a normal part of life.

Stress, like death and taxes, is inevitable. Author and motivator Denis Waitley advises, "One of the best ways to adapt to the many stresses of life is simply to accept them as normal. The adversity and failures in our lives, if we view them as corrective feedback, serve to develop in us an immunity against the adverse responses to stress."

Actually, stress isn't always bad. I have a deadline to finish this book. That puts stress on me to do my job within a reasonable length of time and motivates me to complete my work. Donald A. Tubesing, an educational psychologist and president of Whole Person Associates in Duluth, Minnesota, likens stress to the tension on a violin string. If the string is too taut, it snaps; but if it's too slack, it won't make music.

Generally, stress factors are neutral. What stresses one person doesn't affect another. For example, I can speak to large groups and never get nervous, but I wouldn't be able to utter a note if I were asked to sing before that same crowd. Conversely, my friend Sue can pour out her heart in song in front of a large audience but clutches if she has to pray aloud in a small group. It's your personal reaction to stress, based on your own personality, beliefs, strengths, weaknesses, and attitudes, that causes you to react negatively to stress.

An improper response to stress results in numerous negative symptoms that can attack and lower self-esteem: lack of peace, a quick temper, trouble relaxing or sleeping, complaining. People who are under stress lose their sense of humor and are consistently grouchy. They also suffer from physical symptoms such as headaches, nervous stomach, and fatigue.

Christ's counsel was don't worry, don't fret, and don't borrow trouble. When faced with a stressful situation, we have two alternatives: do something about it if we can or accept it if we can't. Christ cautioned Martha not to be worried and bothered about so many things; He stressed that "each day has enough trouble of its own" (Matthew 6:34).

Adapting Brings Peace

Adapting, rather than trying to force or mold situations, also helps you cultivate peace. In *The Power of Positive Thinking* Dr. Norman Vincent Peale advises, "One of the simplest methods of reducing tension is to practice the easy-does-it attitude. Do everything more slowly, less hectically, and without pressure."

Realistically, you have very little influence over other people's behavior or the structure of the circumstances in which God places you. Trying to force or mold situations or people usually doesn't accomplish much except agitating others and disrupting your peace of mind.

Donna tried for years to pair up her daughter Cindy with her best friend's son, Eric. She contrived social situations, from vacations to barbecues to errand running, hoping to throw the kids together. She did everything within her power to force the situation. She was always agitated about

Cindy's social life and hypercritical of every boy she dated. She was so upset when Cindy got engaged to a boy she met at college, she almost alienated her daughter. She caused an immeasurable amount of unnecessary stress for herself and everyone else concerned. In spite of all her contriving, although Cindy and Eric ended up being good friends, they both married other people.

Adapting is easier once you realize that control is an illusion. Acknowledging that there's no such thing as a "sure thing" helps you let go. Although you can, and should, plan, project, and set goals, ultimately your life is in God's hands and is subject to the sovereign winds of His divine circumstance. In the end, the only control you can successfully apply is self-control. Mothers can't make their children fall in love with someone they've decided would be a perfect mate. All they can do is educate them about how to make wise choices and respect the decisions their adult children make. My son, Brian, can't control which baseball league will draft him, but he can play his best for whatever team chooses him. Sam can't tell the company whom to hire as his supervisor, but he can respect that person's authority and expertise.

The secret to adapting is relaxing in your circumstances, whatever they may be. The apostle Paul is a glowing example of how to relax in your circumstances. He passed the simple secret of his peace on to us. It is, ". . . I have learned to be content in whatever circumstances I am" (Philippians 4:11). Whether he was dining with dignitaries or eating swill in a rat-infested dungeon; whether hungry or well fed, needy or well provided for, Paul experienced God's peace because he relaxed in his circumstances. He did not bemoan, resent, or fight his fate. He simply accepted and rested in God's grace. I don't know about you, but when I'm able to do that, not only am I more peaceful but I like myself better.

Be Resilient

Another way to cultivate peace is to be resilient. You need to learn how to bounce instead of crumbling when you're struck by misfortune and problems. For example, if you drop a china teacup on cement it will shatter into many pieces but bounce a tennis ball and it will spring back higher than the level from which it fell. Things that are rigid and unbending have no resiliency. They break easily when they strike a hard surface.

People who are resilient have pliable, "tennis ball" personalities. They realize that swimming upstream against the current wastes a lot of time and energy; they are able to roll with the flow of life, fit into the ongoing scheme of things, adapt to change, and make allowances for their and other people's mistakes. Consequently, they live relatively stress-free lives and can bounce back when life deals them a hard blow.

Conversely, people who are rigid and unbending crumble under the strain of normal, everyday living. They overreact to inconsequential things such as flat tires, burned toast, and cold coffee. They create a lot of stress for themselves and others. For example, have you ever known anyone who *always* had to be right? Unfortunately, I've known far too many, but Patricia is probably the most intractable of all. The only kind of car anyone should buy is the make she owns; the only brand of toothpaste to use, the only diet to follow, the only way to comb children's hair, the only church to attend, or the only way to cook beef stew, is *her* way. Since no one is always right and very few people think exactly alike, Patricia imposes enormous stress on herself. She suffers from migraine headaches and ulcers and is always in turmoil trying to control what everyone thinks and does.

To cultivate peace you need to be as elastic as a rubber

band that snaps right back into shape when the tension eases, even when it has been stretched to the breaking point.

Becoming a Peacemaker

Jesus taught that we will be happy when we pursue peace; when we make it our life-style. He did not say blessed are the warriors, yet many people live as if He did—even Christians who know better and are indwelt by the Holy Spirit, who is able to produce the fruit of peace in their lives. If you're one of them, you might try applying some of the following peacemaking principles.

Don't attack. If you're a person who is ready to attack when someone threatens you by disagreeing with you or criticizing you, or if you're inclined to do battle to get your own way, you're living a war. I'm reminded of Alice, an excellent teacher, who is driving women away from the Bible study she teaches because she gets so defensive when anyone in the group disagrees with her that she discounts any opinions or insights they share.

I think of Connie, whose immediate response to any criticism, even if it's a constructive, valid one given in love, is to recite a list of what's wrong with the person she sees as her "accuser." She fights with her husband a lot, won't accept his counsel, seems to have no respect for his opinions.

Women like Alice and Connie do not feel good about themselves. Neither will you if you arm yourself with belligerent defensive attitudes and are always ready to attack. Attacking makes enemies, not friends; war, not peace. Attacking diminishes self-esteem because it sets you up for rejection. Normal people retreat when someone is shooting at them.

Compromise. Cultivating peace means you'll need to learn how to compromise and be willing to make concessions; to give up bits and pieces of your way and your will to maintain harmony. An article about the negotiations that took place between a union and its members cited a list of concessions each side made during the negotiations so they could reach an agreement and settle the dispute. Compromise is what peacemaking is about.

Nothing can agitate a person's spirit more than taking a stand and holding a hard line—regardless. I know when I'm dogmatic and unbending, I'm not peaceful. I grit my teeth and the muscles in my neck and shoulders tighten. Gradually, my peace of mind dissipates and anxiety takes its place. You know what I mean; we've all been there.

Women who are not willing or able to make concessions don't feel good about themselves. They heap anxiety on their souls by creating tension with their unbending attitudes. And, they alienate people because they stop communicating with anyone who isn't on "their" side. That detracts from their feelings of self-worth.

Concentrate on your actions and reactions. Instead of being upset about what someone else thinks, says, or does, focus on what you think, say, and do. When you concentrate on your own actions and reactions, you won't be as affected by the attitudes and actions of others, so you'll be more peaceful.

An old adage warns against the danger of becoming your own worst enemy. That's good counsel. Many people court controversy because they are trying so hard to control others that they don't control themselves. To cultivate peace, you need to ask yourself if your participation or response in a situation will cause trouble or bring peace, create chaos or relieve stress. When you do, you'll eliminate a lot of contention and wrangling, so you'll feel better about yourself.

The Best Benefit of All

But the best benefit of pursuing peace is that it helps you see yourself as a child of God who has inherited His beauty and His capacity for loving and accepting yourself and others. Jesus promised, "Blessed are the peacemakers, for they shall be called sons of God" (Matthew 5:9).

When you focus on God, in whose image you are made; you view yourself in a more positive, productive way. You experience a very real sense of His presence and that brings peace.

Being a peacemaker who sees herself as an offspring of the Almighty can't help but improve your self-image, raise your self-esteem, and take you one step closer to becoming God's special woman.

Workshop

Pursuing Peace

I. This exercise will help you determine the present level of your self-esteem. In the space below, write five phrases that most accurately describe how you presently feel about yourself. These can be both positive and negative. They shouldn't be all bad! Then write five phrases that best describe feelings you would like to experience about yourself.

A. How I feel about myself now:

1. _____
2. _____
3. _____
4. _____
5. _____

B. How I would like to feel about myself:

1. _____
2. _____
3. _____
4. _____
5. _____

II. Now, let's look at a scriptural formula for cultivating peace. Read Philippians 4:6, 7 in several translations, then answer these questions.

    1. What situations and people are presently causing anxiety in your life?

_____

_____

2. What is one thing you can do in each instance to cultivate peace? (Be specific and practical. For example, if you're having difficulty communicating with your teenager, don't say, "Be more understanding." Say, "I will listen carefully and try not to be critical of little things that don't matter.")

_____

_____

3. When you pray, do you ask for His guidance and direction or do you tell Him what you think He should do? What does presenting your requests to God actually mean?

_____

_____

4. What does praying with thanksgiving mean? Aren't you being hypocritical if you thank God for something for which you aren't grateful? How can praying with thanks cultivate peace?

_____

_____

_____

5. Refer back to question one, to the list of situations and people that are causing you anxiety and interfering with your peace of mind. How can God's peace guard your heart and mind from these things?

_____

_____

_____

III. In this chapter we discussed qualities that help cultivate peace. This quiz will help you weed out some negatives so you can sow the seeds of self-esteem in their place.

Check the proper response.

Quality	Very much like me	I'm like this sometimes	Not like me at all
1. I get upset easily when faced with a stressful situation.			
2. I do everything I can to avoid any kind of stress.			
3. I try to force or mold situations and people.			
4. I have difficulty relaxing in my circumstances, even if I'm convinced I can do nothing to change them.			
5. I tend to be rather rigid and unbending.			
6. I have difficulty bouncing back when life deals me a blow.			
7. I am inclined to attack or put down people who challenge me or my opinions.			

Quality	Very much like me	I'm like this sometimes	Not like me at all
8. I get defensive when someone criticizes or disagrees with me.			
9. Once I make up my mind, I don't change it.			
10. I generally seem to be involved in some kind of controversy.			
11. I don't think of myself as a peace-maker.			

Now evaluate your answers. If your responses fell mostly in the "very much like me" column, you are being your own worst enemy. You're probably creating a lot of negative stress for yourself and need to work much harder at pursuing peace.

If you checked about an equal number of responses in each column, you recognize your strengths and weaknesses as a peacemaker and know what you have to do to modify the negatives that are disrupting your peace of mind.

If the majority of your answers were in the "not like me at all" category, you probably are a person who already actively pursues peace.

Chapter Six

Acquiring Self-Respect

Another quality you must cultivate to help overcome low self-esteem is *self-respect*. I believe there are two basic reasons why women do not respect themselves. One is that they behave unrighteously; the other is that they judge their worth by externals. In this chapter we'll see how both of those factors detract from self-respect.

Sin is the ultimate image detractor. It is the root cause of numerous other self-image problems because it keeps you from seeing yourself as you really are. It affects self-esteem because it makes you feel lousy about yourself and messes up your relationship with God and others. Sin makes you ugly inside, so it detracts from your dignity and feelings of self-worth. Ultimately, it destroys your self-respect, and your sense of self-esteem will stay low until you deal with the effects of sin in your life.

I did something this fall I've never done in my life. When I cleaned out my closet, I gave away every article of clothing I own, except for four swimsuits and six pairs of shorts, which I wear when I exercise. I got rid completely of my old dresses, skirts, blouses, pants, tee shirts, and jackets. I did so for several reasons. I knew that from that time on I would always think of them as the clothes I wore the summer George died and that I would forever associate them with the places we went and the time we spent together. Hardest of all was that it seemed so ironic that those clothes, inanimate objects I cared nothing about, were still here during the summer but George wasn't. Also, most of them were old and out of style, plus I'd lost almost thirty pounds, so none of them fit. I wanted to start this next summer with a fresh, new wardrobe, to get rid of all the old clothing and start over.

Perhaps Paul had something similar in mind, in a spiritual sense, when he charged us to "put on the new self who is being renewed to a true knowledge according to the image of the One who created him" (Colossians 3:10). Even though we've been created in God's image and recreated in Christ, a lot of us are still wearing outdated, negative opinions and clothing ourselves in unrighteous attitudes and actions that diminish our self-respect. If you're going to become God's special woman, you need to clean out your mental wardrobe and rid yourself of such garments.

Revamping the Wardrobe of Your Soul

I want to share with you a procedure I learned years ago that I still use consistently to help me identify and eliminate the image detractor of sin. I liken this to maintaining a wardrobe. It isn't something you do once and never have to do again or that you can do once in a while. Our souls require constant maintenance. I do laundry almost every day. I'm always sewing on buttons or taking up or letting down hems and removing spots from garments. I regularly discard clothing that is worn out or that I've had so long I'm sick of it and replace it with new items. I employ my "sin list procedure" in a similar way.

I don't know the origin of the procedure—and I've revised it as I've taught it—but I'll be eternally grateful that God gave it to me because it breaks down all barriers of self-deceit and forces me to uncover and acknowledge traits of my old self and to see my sin for what it is. Doing it isn't easy, but it results in great blessing. I promise, if you are willing to use it and stick with it, you'll be transformed and feel better about yourself than you ever have. Every time I teach this "sin-list procedure" miracles occur. I have seen relationships restored, buried guilt unearthed and relinquished, and emotional, spiritual, and physical healings take place. Through the years I've learned that whenever I start to slip spiritually, or when I start feeling badly about myself or get critical of others, it's time to use this procedure because there's a build-up of the old self that needs to be exorcised.

The Four Cs of Cleansing

The sin-list procedure consists of four simple steps: Clarifying the meaning of sin; Considering your ways; Confessing your sin; and Claiming your cleansed position in Christ. The first step in this cleansing is to clarify the meaning of sin. Each of you has your own concept of sin. If you're going to identify and eliminate it, you need to define it from God's perspective. There are eight Greek words in the New Testament for sin. Examining them will help you understand God's view of sin.

The first word is found in Romans 4:25: "Who [Jesus our Lord] was delivered for our *offenses*, and was raised again for our justification" (KJV, italics mine). This word *offenses*, is usually translated "transgression" and means that sin is falling when you should have stood upright. You fall when you give in to temptation. Adam and Eve fell in the Garden.

The second word for sin is found in Romans 5:14: "Nevertheless death reigned from Adam until Moses, even over those who had not sinned in the likeness of the *offense* of Adam." Here the Greek paints a picture of overstepping bounds; the sin of going beyond that fine line that God draws between right and wrong, good and evil, sin and righteousness.

A third term used for sin in Romans 5:19 relates to hearing: "For as through the one man's *disobedience* the many were made sinners, even so through the obedience of the One the many will be made righteous." This kind of sin involves refusing to listen to God as well as disobeying what you have heard; actively going against His stated, known will.

In 1 John 3:4, the word *sin* means "lawlessness": "Everyone who practices sin also practices lawlessness; and sin is lawlessness." It depicts us as spiritual renegades who don't keep God's commandments or maintain His standards. We are lawbreakers; spiritual criminals.

The fifth Greek word used for sin in the New Testament is found in Romans 1:18 and describes sin as godlessness: "For the wrath of God is revealed from heaven against all ungodliness and unrighteousness of men, who suppress the truth in unrighteousness." This is the sin of withholding from God the praise, worship, adoration, and reverence He deserves. You commit this sin when you shut Him out and give other gods a place in your life.

A sixth form of sin is described in 1 Timothy 1:13: "I was formerly a blasphemer and a persecutor and a violent aggressor. And yet I was shown mercy, because I acted ignorantly in unbelief." This is the sin of transgressing because you do not act in faith or you haven't learned God's commandments so you can keep them. But, as in human affairs, ignorance of God's law is no excuse. It is your responsibility to find out what He expects from you and to do it.

James 4:17 describes the sin of omission: "To one who knows the right thing to do, and does not do it, to him it is sin." This is failing to do what you should have done; withholding yourself, your love, or your services; quenching the Spirit. Instead of doing wrong, this is not doing what is right and required.

The Greek word *hamartia* is used more frequently than any other in Scripture to describe sin. It means missing the mark and was originally used to describe an archer shooting an arrow and missing the target. One of the best-known verses using this word is Romans 3:23. "For all have sinned and fall short of the glory of God." We simply do not live up to all God created us to be. We fall short of His design and expectations.

Consider Your Ways!

Sin certainly has many faces. But a general knowledge of sin isn't sufficient to cleanse and change you. Once you understand what sin is, you need to examine yourself and identify its active presence in your life. The second step in the sin-list procedure is to follow the Lord's admonition in Haggai 1:7, "Consider your ways!" When you examine yourself, you see your sin, become sensitive to it, and are able to forsake it and put on the new self. David verified, "I considered my ways, And turned my feet to Thy testimonies" (Psalms 119:59).

This step is designed to help you consider your ways. I suggest you pray before you read each of the following Scriptures. Ask the Lord to reveal your sin to you as you examine yourself in the light of His Word. Read each Scripture slowly, in several translations, so you can digest the full meaning of what God is saying to you. As the Spirit reveals His truth to you, write whatever He brings to your mind in each category. You may need to spend several hours doing this. Don't rush into the presence of God; linger at the throne of grace. Give Him a chance to show you yourself as you really are.

Read Matthew 6:33. Consider all the things you've put first before God; things you've loved, sought, or placed ahead of the Lord, such as personal comfort and pleasures, work, family, friends, or church. _____

_____

_____

Read James 4:1. Recall ways you've failed to submit to God, when you've exerted your will over His and said, "Not Thy will but mine." _____

_____

_____

Read 1 John 2:15–17. Think of all the areas of your life that are tinged with worldliness. Consider the literature you read, the music you listen to, your television-viewing habits, places and methods of amusement, friends, and evidence of immodesty or arrogance in the way you dress or act. _____

_____

_____

Read Matthew 22:39. Ask God to help you remember all of the ways you've broken Christ's supreme law of love toward others, such as being envious, critical, impatient, unforgiving, judgmental, or resentful. _____

_____

_____

Read Matthew 5:23–25. Ask God to point out situations where you should make restitution; problems (past or present) that must be made right and settled, in your family, marriage, friendships, church, place of employment, and business transactions. This may range from changing your attitude, offering a simple apology, to confessing and asking forgiveness of someone. _____

_____

_____

Read Philippians 2:3–5. Try to identify all of the ways you glorify self: self-pity, self-satisfaction, self-righteousness, defensiveness, willfulness, touchiness, and selfishness. Consider all of the ways in which you demand your own way and exert yourself and your welfare over that of others.

_____

_____

_____

Confess Your Sins

If you're reacting like I do when I use this procedure, you're probably feeling ashamed, guilty, and dirty right now. That's good. Christians should feel deep sorrow for their sins. But wallowing in them doesn't remove them. The reason you need to identify these old self sin patterns in your life is so you can get rid of them. You do that by *confessing* them; by acknowledging your transgressions before God, and turning them over to Him. First John 1:9 promises that "if we confess our sins, He is faithful and righteous to forgive us our sins and to cleanse us from all unrighteousness."

Confession is more than saying "I'm sorry" to God. It is naming your sins in His presence and claiming His cleansing as you do. True confession involves calling your sins by their proper names. With God, you can't say you "stretched the truth," you have to say you lied and that you are a liar. You can't rationalize to Him and say, I was rude to Jane today because she criticized the Bible lesson I taught last week. You have to say, I was rude to Jane—*period*. No excuses.

Now read back through the list of sins you identified in

step two. Confess them all—every failure, impurity, and shortcoming. Ask God to reveal any unknown sin, any areas where you are deceiving yourself, then to cleanse those hidden corners of your heart. When you finish, thank Him for forgiving you.

Some of you may never have prayed this intensely before. This kind of confession demands a lot and should make you sense the absolute horror of sin. It will stir you physically and emotionally. You may shake or cry. That's fine. Contrition sometimes brings tears of regret and relief. But this kind of deep, heartfelt confession leads to true repentance.

Repent!

Repentance is the fourth step in the cleansing process. Confession helps you get rid of your old wardrobe (the old self); repentance is like putting on the new. Repenting means you "consider yourselves to be dead to sin, but alive to God in Christ Jesus" (Romans 6:11).

Think for a moment about what being dead to sin means. Something that is dead is lifeless and unresponsive. Dead bodies don't move; they aren't affected by the stimuli that affected them when they were alive. Considering yourself dead to sin means you can be totally unresponsive to it. You simply refuse to "wear" it any longer, just as you do the outdated, worn-out clothes in your wardrobe.

You'll be amazed at how much better you feel about yourself once you remove the image detractor of sin and put on that new self. Your cleansed soul will exude a fresh, inner beauty. You'll like and respect the reflection you see when you look into the mirror of self. You'll recognize one of God's special women. Eventually you'll learn to respect yourself for what you are, not for what you own, accomplish, or look like.

Don't Judge Your Worth by Externals

Many women do not respect themselves because they judge their worth by externals. This is especially prevalent in today's society. Every self-image book I have read discusses how destructive the superficial standards of beauty, intelligence, affluence, and accomplishment are to a person's self-worth. Consequently, if a woman isn't highly educated, or supersmart, or doesn't have money, nice clothes, and an expensive home, or a successful, upwardly mobile career, or is physically blemished in some way (and who isn't?), she loses respect for herself.

God's Word cautions women about depending on externals to validate their worth. Peter advised, "Let not your adornment be merely external—braiding the hair, and wearing gold jewelry, or putting on dresses; but let it be the hidden person of the heart, with the imperishable quality of a gentle and quiet spirit, which is so precious in the sight of God" (1 Peter 3:3, 4). In God's eyes, external beauty—what you look like—is no indicator of your worth.

Neither are possessions and accomplishments. God accepts you apart from your works, just as you are, and you'll lose respect for yourself if you don't do the same. Dr. J. Allan Petersen stresses that "self-esteem [must] not [be] based on the great things you've accomplished, the mark you've made, the things you own" (*Two Become One*, Tyndale, 1973, p. 30). Dr. David Burns believes that "self-worth based on accomplishment is *pseudo-esteem;* not the genuine thing" (*Reader's Digest*, March, 1985).

In an article in *Partnership* magazine, Mary Ellen Ton vividly described the crisis she faced when she lost those superficial, external validators. She was badly burned over 55 percent of her body in a fire at the church where she worked. Her face was severely disfigured, her hands twisted and deformed. "All the physical attributes that had helped to clothe my self-esteem were suddenly stripped away. Everything that had seemed a vital part of my self-image was gone. I didn't even look human. Little children were afraid of me. I felt I had lost my humanity and would never again be able to function as a normal person" ("No Longer Beautiful," *Partnership*, June, 1985, p. 37).

We can only imagine the horror Mary Ellen experienced. But somehow, with tremendous faith and courage, she has managed to maintain her self-respect. She explains, "I . . . have to continually exercise my self-esteem. Living with burn scars, I have to continually stretch the good images I have of myself. I have to daily remind myself that I am created in the image of God; that makes me unique and valuable. I listen intently to what my family and friends tell me about myself. I accept their affirmations of love and their expressions of pride in me. I turn the volume down as quickly as possible on the negative messages that daily bombard me in a society where physical attractiveness is equated with a woman's value. I affirm myself for those things I do well. I forgive myself for not being perfect. I accept all compliments."

How to Cultivate Self-Respect

What an example to us all! Mary Ellen learned how to cultivate self-respect against odds few, if any of you, will ever have to face. If she did it, you can, too. Let's look at some simple suggestions that will help you respect yourself for what you are, rather than judging your worth by externals.

One: Concentrate on what matters. Don't ignore externals but don't dwell on them either. Be more concerned with who you are (your character and moral values) than with what you can do. When you concentrate on superficial externals, you lose self-respect and your self-esteem ebbs.

Two: Accept and appreciate your God-created uniqueness. Many women lose respect for themselves because they think of differences as drawbacks. Actually, they are part of the Lord's distinctive handiwork and add spice and dimension to our lives. Imagine how dull and drab life would be if everyone looked, thought, and felt the same; if there was no color in nature—only black and white.

Thinking of differences as flaws or liabilities focuses you on externals. This forces you to make comparisons—prettier, thinner, smarter, luckier, happier—so you lose self-respect. Remember, of the more than three and one-half billion people on this earth no two are exactly alike! Each individual is a testimony to God's creativity and love of diversity. Contrary to popular opinion, uniformity is not a virtue. If God had wanted us all to be alike, He would have designed us that way. Instead, He designed us so we can express our God-created differences through our individuality.

Three: Never do anything that is against your principles. Be true to yourself. Do what you believe is right, fair, moral, and good. When you compromise your beliefs, you lose self-respect.

Four: Never do anything that is against God's standards. You pay a price when you deliberately disobey the Lord; it costs you your self-respect.

Five: Practice self-control. Control your passions instead of letting them control you. Paul said, ". . . All things are lawful for me, but I will not be mastered by anything" (1 Corinthians 6:12). When you lose control of your thoughts and actions, you also lose self-respect.

Six: Live by the Golden Rule. Anything you do that detracts from the worth of others detracts from you, too. "Little" people belittle others; godly women edify and encourage people by treating them with courtesy and respect. You cannot respect yourself unless you show respect to others.

In his poem "Myself," poet Edgar A. Guest summed up the attitude of self-respect that can help us more fully become God's special women.

> *I have to live with myself, and so. . . .*
> *I don't want to stand with the setting sun*
> *And hate myself for the things I've done. . . .*
> *I want to go out with my head erect,*
> *I want to deserve all men's respect. . . .*
> *Whatever happens I want to be*
> *Self-respecting and conscience free.*

Workshop

Acquiring Self-Respect

I. Read again each New Testament definition of sin and the corresponding Scripture. Write one way each type of sin manifests itself in your life; then write a sentence telling how that sin detracts from your self-respect. Use the sin-list procedure for confessing these sins to the Lord.

1. _____

2. _____

3. _____

4. _____

5. _____

6. _____

7. _____

8. _____

II. This exercise will help you determine what you need to do to cultivate a deeper sense of self-respect.

A. Are you concentrating on what matters or are you judging your worth by externals? In the chart below list five externals you use to judge your worth by. Beside each one write a character asset or moral value you possess that you would still have left if you lost the external quality, as Mary Ellen Ton did. Then write a sentence telling one thing you can do to improve or enhance every quality you listed.

External	Enhance-ment	Internal	Enhance-ment
1.			
2.			
3.			
4.			
5.			

B. What's your attitude about your God-created differences? Are you diminishing your self-respect by comparing yourself to others?

   1. Read each of the following statements about differences, then write a sentence telling why you agree or disagree with it.

      a) "You [should be] thankful to God for how He made you (big ears, long nose and all). You don't waste time wishing you were tall and willowy rather than short or a bit on the chunky side. You don't argue with God about why He seemed to make so many beautiful and talented people, while He made you rather plain and average" (Fritz Ridenour, *Lord, What's Really Important?*, Regal, 1978).

      _____

      _____

      _____

      _____

      b) "It seems safe to assume that God enjoys variety. . . . In His famous speech in the Book of Job, God pointed with pride to [the] oddities of crea-

124

tion" (Dr. Paul Brand and Philip Yancey, *Fearfully and Wonderfully Made*, Zondervan, 1980).

_____

_____

_____

_____

c) "God did not create any superior or inferior people. There are only different people. Abilities and capacities differ; each person has unique strengths which enable him to make his special contribution to God's plan" (*Two Become One*, J. Allan Petersen, Tyndale, 1973).

_____

_____

_____

_____

2. Now, list three ways you are uniquely different from any other person. Write a reason why you should be grateful for and respect each difference.

Difference	Appreciation
a)	
b)	
c)	

C. Each of us has a set of moral values, a code of ethics, by which we live. In the space below list five principles you believe you must adhere to to maintain your self-respect. Think about, then write what you can do to comply more closely with each belief.

	Principle	Enhancement
a)		
b)		
c)		
d)		
e)		

D. How well do you practice self-control? List three "passions" or bad habits that tend to master you and decrease your self-respect; then write one thing you can do to control each.

	Habit	Plan for Overcoming
a)		
b)		
c)		

Chapter Seven

Be All That You Can Be

Although you should not judge your worth based on your performance or accomplishments, you should try to be all that you can be; to do your best in any task God sets before you, whether cleaning toilets or managing a corporation. To do that you'll need to cultivate *proficiency*. Proficiency—which is learning to do things easily, competently, and well—elevates self-esteem because it overcomes the image detractors of inefficiency, inadequacy, and inferiority, and develops efficiency, confidence, and improves your performance. Cultivating proficiency involves fine tuning your skills, adding to your knowledge, and learning how to best develop and use your abilities. You don't have to be highly educated or superintelligent to develop proficiency, but you must be willing to do everything you can to do the best possible job.

I have spent over four decades learning my craft—writing. Words are the tools of my trade, so to be proficient I had to learn how to handle the English language. I must know the parts of speech and how to use them, how to spell and punctuate, use a dictionary, incorporate synonyms and antonyms into a text, and how to present ideas simply and clearly.

I constantly meet people who tell me they want to be writers and who ask me to look over something they have written. Almost without exception their manuscripts are full of misspelled words, typographical errors, run-on sentences, split infinitives, dangling participles, and tenses that don't agree. Usually I correct one or two paragraphs, then return the material with a letter telling them they must learn how to handle the language if they want to write salable material. Editors look for and buy polished professional manuscripts.

I am not a proficient writer because my IQ goes off the chart or because I'm exceptionally insightful, but because I do my homework (research) and I know how to use words properly.

The headline of a recent article in the *Los Angeles Times* caught my eye: "THE KEY TO SUCCESS? It's Drive, Not Talent, Study Finds." Education writer David G. Savage reported, "A five-year study of 120 of the nation's top artists, athletes and scholars has concluded that drive and determination, not great natural talent, led to their extraordinary success.

" 'We expected to find tales of great natural gifts,' said University of Chicago education professor Benjamin Bloom, who led the team of researchers who studied the careers of America's top performers in six fields: concert pianists, Olympic swimmers, sculptors, tennis players, mathematicians, and research neurologists."

What researchers did find was that these superstars, who

were rarely the best in their school classes and often appeared not to be physically or mentally qualified, succeeded because they cultivated proficiency. Practice and motivation determined their success.

The study showed that these ordinary people developed into extraordinary achievers because of their desire to be good at what they did. "A child would practice the piano several hours daily for 17 years to attain his goal of becoming a concert pianist. A typical swimmer would tell of getting up at 5:30 every morning to swim two hours before school and then two hours after school to attain his or her goal of making the Olympic team" (*Los Angeles Times*, February 17, 1985).

Three Key Factors

I believe there are three key factors that help us cultivate proficiency: enthusiasm, optimism, and creativity. Ralph Waldo Emerson noted that "nothing great was ever achieved without enthusiasm." Movie pioneer Samuel Goldwyn believed that "enthusiasm is the key not only to the achievement of great things but to the accomplishment of anything that is worthwhile." Paul counseled, "Whatsoever ye do, do it heartily . . ." (Colossians 3:23 KJV).

I have always enjoyed keeping house, and I am sure the main reason is that my mother was such an enthusiastic example. She never said we *have* to clean house but rather, today you *get* to help me clean. I remember after she would dust a piece of furniture she'd step back, admire her work, and say, "My, just look at how that shines." Or, when she would do laundry (for the first several years of my life in an old, wringer-type washer, before the days of detergents and prewash products), she would say, "See how white those sheets are and how good they smell!"

In the original Greek language of the New Testament the word *heartily* means "out of the soul." Enthusiasm is a fervor and zeal which springs from deep within our souls. That internal exuberance is part of our godlikeness and has its root in the words *en + theos*, which mean "in God." Enthusiasm is God's energy spilling out of our souls!

Enthusiasm gives meaning to even the most mundane of tasks. It makes hard work seem like play and motivates us to do a job well. Auto pioneer Henry Ford, who was laughed at and told his newfangled contraption would never replace the horse and buggy, said, "You can do anything if you have enthusiasm. Enthusiasm is the yeast that makes your hopes rise to the stars. Enthusiasm is the sparkle in your eyes, the swing in your gait, the grip of your hand, the irresistible surge of will and energy to execute your ideas.

"Enthusiasts are fighters. They have fortitude. They have staying qualities. Enthusiasm is at the bottom of all progress. With it, there is accomplishment. Without it, there are only alibis."

An Attitude of Optimism

Optimism is the second key factor in cultivating proficiency. Optimism is an inclination to apply favorable connotations and to anticipate the best possible outcome. Unfortunately, too many Christians, who have every reason to be optimistic (if God is for us who can be against us?) are soothsayers of gloom. They may quote, "I can do all things through [Christ] who strengthens me" (Philippians 4:13), but they believe and act as if that truth applies to everyone but them. They say "I can't" instead of "I'll try," "I'm afraid" instead of "I'll trust." That kind of defeatist attitude lowers self-esteem.

There is only one way to develop an optimistic attitude and that is to take God at His word. I've isolated three reasons why Christians are pessimistic. The first is habit. They are accustomed to thinking pessimistically; to looking for the worst instead of expecting the best, and have conditioned themselves to expect the worst, probably to keep from getting hurt. As one wife recently told me, "If I don't expect my husband to invest the time and thoughtfulness required to buy me a birthday or anniversary present, then I'm not disappointed when he hands me a twenty-dollar bill and tells me to go buy myself something." (She later admitted she was lying to herself—she *is* disappointed every time that happens.)

I asked her what she thought would happen if she handed the money back to him and told him she preferred he buy the gift himself. Her pessimistic reply was, "Oh, he'd say he doesn't know what to get me or doesn't have the time."

So I pressed her further and asked what would happen if she gave him some suggestions and told him it would make her very happy if he took the time to buy her a gift. She shrugged her shoulders and said, "I doubt I'd get anything."

Although she may be right, that woman has a habit of thinking pessimistically. I know several women in similar situations who have been willing not to jump to conclusions and who have been able to remedy the situation by applying a little positive, friendly persuasion.

It Looks Hopeless to Me!

Another reason why Christians are pessimistic is that they look at and for negatives rather than positives. I was watching an old movie on television the other night. A small group of people had survived an airplane crash by swimming to the shore of a deserted island. As is always the case in that kind of drama, a strong, authoritative man, named Ralph, took charge and started organizing the survivors. He gave everyone instructions. "Ann, you gather grass to make beds; Sam, you gather tree leaves to weave into blankets; Ben, you take Sue and Tom and gather firewood and look for food."

Ben balked as he pulled a soggy book of matches from his shirt pocket and threw it on the sand. "What good will that do? All of the matches are wet."

The hero asked if anyone had a cigarette lighter. Alas, Tom, Ann, and Sam didn't smoke. Sue did, but her lighter was in her purse, which was long gone with the tide. Undeterred, Ralph picked up the matches Ben had discarded and studied them. "Look! There are a couple in the middle that aren't ruined."

Ben mumbled something about the impossibility of lighting a campfire with them, to which Ralph replied, "It only takes one match to start a fire, and we have two. Now, let's get busy." What a hero!

That melodramatic scene is a perfect illustration of how an optimist and a pessimist, when faced with an identical set of circumstances, approach the situation. Many people are Bens. They don't assess the overall situation but instead isolate and dwell on the negatives. They look for bad instead of good, for impossibilities instead of possibilities, at the trap they feel they are in instead of the way out. Eventually they lose hope and develop a pessimistic attitude toward everything and everyone, including themselves. Their self-esteem suffers.

Optimism cultivates self-esteem because it affects outcomes. When you look for good, you usually find it. When you believe there is a solution to a problem, even if you do not know what it is, you look for ways to solve that problem and end up overcoming it. When you hope for and try your best, you succeed, or at least accomplish *something*. When you look for light instead of groping in darkness, you move toward the Son.

Sharpening Creativity

The third key factor that can help you cultivate proficiency is *creativity*. In her book *Ms. Means Myself* (Zondervan, 1972, p. 59), Gladys Hunt defines creativity as "taking the stuff of life that exists and shaping it." Gail Sheehy, author of the books *Passages* and *Pathfinders*, says "Creativity could be described as letting go of certainties" (*Pathfinders*, William Morrow, 1981, p. 97).

You will feel inferior if you do not develop creativity or use your ingenuity. I once heard the story about a news reporter, an architect, and a sculptor. Each was asked to give his impression of a huge boulder. The reporter said, "It is a forty-by-sixty-foot, indestructible piece of granite." The architect said, "It is a permanent part of the landscape which cannot be moved." But the sculptor said, "It is the raw material from which I create beauty as I reshape it with my hammer and chisel."

Too many people approach life and its inherent difficulties as if it were an indestructible piece of granite. Others view it as an immovable force that blocks the path they want to take. But the innovative sculptors among us look at life as the raw material from which they can create beauty and, with God's help, reshape with the hammer and chisel of creativity.

William Bernbach noted that "an idea can turn to dust or magic, depending on the talent that rubs against it." Creativity develops proficiency because it helps you look at life from a different perspective and challenges you to look for innovative solutions to seemingly insurmountable problems and so keeps you from giving up or seeing yourself as a failure. Consequently, your self-esteem rises and you move forward toward becoming God's special woman.

Workshop

Be All That You Can Be

I. This workshop will help you evaluate ways in which you are proficient and help you spot areas where you need to improve. On the chart below, in column A, list five things you do easily, competently, and well; then write what you had to do to become proficient in that area. In column B, list five things you have to do or want to do that are difficult for you; then write one thing you might do to develop proficiency in each area.

A		B	
Task	Skills	Task	Skills

II. Now let's examine the proficiency factors in your life. Complete each sentence. (Cross out the appropriate word or phrase where necessary.)

1. One area where I feel inadequate is _____

_____.

2. One way I feel inferior to most people is _____

_____.

3. I (believe, do not believe) I can do anything I set my mind to, that practice and hard work (can, cannot) determine my success because _____.

4. I find I am most enthusiastic when _____

_____.

5. I cannot be enthusiastic about _____

because _____.

6. I would describe myself as an (optimist, pessimist) because _____

_____

7. I am most optimistic when _____

_____

8. I am most pessimistic when _____

_____

9. Three ways I am creative are _____

_____.

10. The proficiency factor I most need to cultivate is

_____

_____ because _____

_____.

Chapter Eight

Becoming Vulnerable

Before reading this chapter, pause a moment and evaluate how you're progressing. Is your self-image better, your self-esteem higher, than when you started working your way through this book? Are you feeling better about yourself? Good! Don't stop now. It's time to cultivate another quality that can further your quest for becoming God's special woman: *Vulnerability*.

Vulnerability is a willingness to be open and honest; to confront and disclose ourselves to others. Many people aren't willing to become vulnerable because they know if they do, they run the risk of being attacked, criticized, misunderstood, misquoted, rejected, misused, or hurt. And that's true. Such dangers exist, but the pleasure we experience when we fully, actively participate in life far outweighs the pain. Better to face a few problems than to be plagued with guilt or regret over missed opportunities. Better to develop endurance by being doers of the Word than to become passive observers whose faith is anemic.

Fear of vulnerability is both a symptom and a cause of low self-esteem. In their book *Women in Mid-Life Crisis*, Jim and Sally Conway observe that it is symptomatic because "a person with low self-image is ... afraid to risk, afraid to speak, because she might experience more hurt" (Tyndale, 1983, p. 208). So low self-esteem causes you to wall yourself off from others to protect and preserve what little esteem you do have. Lack of vulnerability *causes* low self-esteem because it keeps you from knowing and expressing yourself. Dr. Lester Keiser noted that "we get so much in the habit of wearing a disguise before others that we eventually appear disguised before ourselves."

Marriage is one area where withholding yourself and lack of vulnerability is most evident and destructive. Many wives are afraid to share their feelings or opinions with their husbands. The reasons they cite are too numerous to mention but they all come under the heading of fear. For example, Connie didn't speak up when her husband cheated on their income-tax return because she was afraid she would make him mad. She signed the form so was equally guilty of dishonesty. Phyllis wore her hair long but was always complaining about how much she hated the style, yet she would not tell her husband how she felt because she was certain he "loved" her more with long hair.

Jane was miserably unhappy at the church she and John were attending but she didn't tell him because she was afraid he would think her reasons for wanting to change were petty. The truth was, an influential woman in the congregation was undermining her ministry, but instead of sharing her frustrations and hurt with her husband, she simply stopped serving on the Mission Committee and teaching Sunday school. Each of those women lost self-esteem because she was afraid to cultivate vulnerability by being open and honest with her mate.

Fear of vulnerability can also affect a woman's attitudes about marriage and her choice of a mate. In an article, "The Incurably Single Woman," (*Los Angeles Times*, February 3, 1985) Linda Marsa wrote that her research showed that the type of woman who does not have a realistic picture of herself "has real fears of intimacy and sends out signals that she doesn't feel that relationships have any real value. . . . The flip side of this coin is . . . the woman unerringly picks men who have trouble written all over them . . . she consistently picks unsuitable partners that, in the final analysis, pose no real threat."

Frightening as it may be, becoming vulnerable raises self-esteem because it breaks down communication barriers, forces you to examine the truth about yourself, and enables you to improve and enrich relationships.

Disclosing Yourself

To cultivate vulnerability you must be willing to disclose yourself to others; to share your hurts and heartaches, fears and concerns; to show affection, express joy and sorrow, state your opinions, and speak the truth in love. For extroverts like me, this is easy. But for "private" people, who have conditioned themselves not to show emotion or share their thoughts and feelings, self-disclosure is extremely threatening and difficult. But not doing so can hinder their emotional development and debilitate self-esteem.

In his book *The Transparent Self*, psychologist Sidney Jourard relates some illuminating information about a study he did on self-disclosure. His major finding was that the human personality has a natural, built-in inclination to reveal itself. His conclusion was that "when that inclination is blocked and we close ourselves to others, we get into emotional difficulties" (quoted in *The Friendship Factor*, Alan Loy McGinnis, Augsburg, 1979, p. 28), one of which is a low sense of self-esteem.

It seems that the need to communicate ourselves to others is normal and natural. God endowed us with emotions and intellect, and the means to express our thoughts and feelings: language, laughter, and tears. Only human beings can laugh, talk, and cry. The way God created us implies that He meant for us to communicate ourselves to others. An inability or unwillingness to do so can cause all sorts of problems—as in Linda and Chuck's marriage.

Chuck claims he can't compliment Linda or tell her he loves her. He says she should know he loves her or he wouldn't stay married to her, and that she should know he likes her cooking and the way she keeps house and the way she wears her hair because he never complains about the meals she serves, the way the house looks, or her appearance. Because he is unwilling or unable to verbalize his feelings, Linda questions his love. All of the subtle things he does to show his love are negated in her mind because he refuses to say, "I love you." Perhaps someday he'll understand why he is so afraid to share his feelings, even with his own wife, but until he is willing to disclose himself, he is seriously jeopardizing his marriage.

A lack of vulnerability, burying or not expressing your thoughts and feelings, can also result in physical problems. People who bottle up their emotions are more prone to heart attacks, ulcers, and even cancer. They've recently been dubbed "C-Type" personalities by cancer specialists.

Why Can't We Disclose Ourselves?

If self-disclosure is normal, natural, and emotionally healthy, why do so many people have trouble communicating themselves to others? I believe there are three major reasons. One is that they do not understand the essence of self-disclosure. They think that disclosing oneself means revealing all sorts of private, intimate details about themselves and their lives to anyone who will listen. Disclosing yourself doesn't mean you have to make your life an open book or tell "all" or that you have to tell everyone everything about yourself. Self-disclosure at its best is revealing your personality, character, and values through the way you live; it is being ready to give and receive love, to welcome others into your life.

A second reason why people do not disclose themselves is that they are afraid of being rejected, ridiculed, or seeming foolish. Susan loved Daniel but she couldn't bring herself to tell him, even when he told her how much he cared for her, because she was afraid he'd reject her. Her coldness drove him away. Amy, a bright young woman who graduated with honors from college, would not share her ideas in planning meetings at her new job for fear she'd be ridiculed. Instead, she shared them in private with her colleagues who were more than willing to pass them on and take credit for them. Judy stifled her wonderful sense of humor for years because she didn't want to seem foolish by clowning around. Fear of vulnerability cost each of those women a goodly portion of self-esteem.

A third reason why people don't self-disclose is that they are trained not to. In our society we perpetuate the myth that strong people, especially men, don't cry. Or that it's unladylike to laugh. Or that it's rude to say what you think. Or that it's sinful to express anger or admit that you don't like someone. Or that overtly showing love, such as openly hugging or kissing friends and relatives, is in bad taste. No wonder we have difficulty communicating! We've been taught not to. We're afraid!

Set Fear Aside

That is why, to cultivate vulnerability, you're going to have to set fear aside and deprogram the automatic reaction to withhold. For example, last night after dinner I drank half a cup of coffee. I didn't want the rest, so I pushed the cup away. It was still on the table, the coffee was still in it, but I didn't drink it. Instead I set it aside.

Similarly, if you are afraid to share your opinions, push the fear away and speak. If you are afraid of failing or looking foolish, set that fear aside and plunge ahead. Becoming vulnerable doesn't negate fear; it means you refuse to be immobilized by it. Christian physician and psychotherapist Paul Tournier noted, "The adventurous life is not one exempt from fear, but on the contrary one that is lived in full knowledge of fears of all kinds; one in which we go forward in spite of our fears."

If anyone ever had reason to be fearful, it was Helen Keller. We take our senses for granted. Few of us ever think about how frightening it must be not to be able to see, hear, or verbally communicate our needs. We all know how Helen set fear aside and went on to become one of the most respected women in history. Helen, who was noted for her wit and wisdom as well as courage, had this to say about vulnerability: "Security is mostly a superstition. It does not exist in nature, nor do the children of men as a whole experience it. Avoiding danger is no safer in the long run than outright exposure. Life is either a daring adventure or nothing."

Be Empathetic

But setting fear aside isn't enough. To fully experience that daring adventure called life you have to be willing to empathize with others, to share both their hurts and joys. Empathy is the capacity for experiencing as one's own the feelings of another. It isn't saying, "If I were you, this is how I would feel." It isn't telling someone how *you* feel about their situation, or how they *should* feel. It is saying, "I am feeling what you are feeling because you are feeling it."

Lewis B. Smedes concluded that when you hurt with hurting people, you are dancing to the rhythm of God. Halford E. Luccock said, "Empathy is your pain in my heart." But he could just as well have said empathy is your joy, or your excitement, or your pride, or your embarrassment in my heart. When we empathize, we identify with whatever others are feeling, be it joy or sorrow, pleasure or pain.

Empathizing cultivates self-esteem because it eliminates the weeds of selfishness and insensitivity. Identifying with the pain and problems, cares and concerns of others helps you understand and relate better to them. You'll feel better about yourself when you feel *for* others. In his book *How Can It Be All Right When Everything Is All Wrong?* Lewis B. Smedes explains that empathy elevates self-esteem because it cements you to Christ. "When I get inside the life of another person, and feel her pain with her, I am on track with the ultimate meaning and power of the universe. Never mind that I do it poorly. Never mind that I don't like doing it at all. When I stick with the outrage of another's pain, I have joined Jesus" (Harper and Row, 1982, p. 68).

How to Empathize

Cultivating empathy is neither difficult nor complicated. First, you need to *tune in.* Forget completely about yourself and how you're feeling and concentrate on the other person. Tuning in on people is like tuning in a radio station. You turn the dial until you get the right frequency, then fine tune until you get a clear signal and there's absolutely no static or interference. In the same way listen carefully to identify and assimilate the feelings the person is sending.

Study facial expressions, body language, and observe moods. Assess and then minister to unstated needs. Don't wait to respond until someone tells you how they are feeling or is forced to ask for help.

Match Moods

A second technique for cultivating empathy is to *match moods*. Paul said we should "rejoice with those who rejoice, and weep with those who weep" (Romans 12:15). When people are happy, you take the edge off their joy if you do not rejoice with them, regardless of how you are feeling personally. When someone is hurting, your first tendency may be to try to stop the pain (most likely because you don't like to see them suffer and you feel helpless) by pointing out positives or quoting Scripture. When people are depressed an immediate reaction is to try to cheer them. That is not empathy. In a way, refusing to experience people's feelings with them is like saying they do not have a right to feel that way. It is a form of denial.

Empathy should be your initial reaction and response to another person's emotions, whatever they may be: joy, grief, anger, frustration. There is, of course, a time and place for positive input, but that comes later. Since George died, the people who have helped me most are those who have carried the burden of my grief by hurting with me. It's as if when they empathize with my sorrow and loneliness, they lift some of it from me and I feel better. The sadness isn't so intense; the grief isn't quite so consuming.

Conversely, some people have burdened and depressed me further by trying to encourage me, instead of empathizing with my discouragement. For the first few months after George died, I felt like I'd been hit in the midsection and had the breath knocked out of me whenever well-meaning but insensitive people would quote Romans 8:28 or tell me they were certain that one positive about my losing my husband was that someday the Lord would have me write a book about widowhood. Those people's efforts, however well-intentioned, added to my pain. I needed them to weep with me when I was weeping, not to tell me to stop crying.

Mood matching keeps you from further hurting people who are in pain or from detracting from their happiness. It affirms joy and helps heal hurts. It is an integral part of becoming vulnerable.

Take Risks

So is *taking risks.* Taking risks cultivates vulnerability and elevates self-esteem because it helps you develop hidden potential. When you try new things, you find out what you can do. You'll learn how to overcome obstacles and become a survivor. In her book *Pathfinders: Overcoming the Crises of Adult Life and Finding Your Own Path to Well-Being*, Gail Sheehy notes that "Women of high well-being usually have confronted a difficulty, rocked the boat, picked themselves up and taken the painful steps necessary to free themselves from what they finally perceived as a trap, self-made or imposed . . . They gain a *great* boost in self-esteem from having taken the risk and having sprung themselves from the trap" (William Morrow, 1981, p. 82).

You'll never know what you can do unless you try. You may surprise yourself and unleash all sorts of untapped resources. Molly did. She had never been employed. She devoted herself to being a wife and mother. Then her husband, Todd, was in a horrible automobile accident that left him debilitated for months. His insurance and the disability plan where he worked supplied about half of their usual income and paid 80 percent of the medical bills. They tried not to dip into their savings but with three children (ages six, eight, and eleven) to feed and clothe, and mortgage, car, and the usual installment payments, they were afraid they would be forced to deplete their nest egg, and still not have enough money to survive.

As a final, desperate move, Molly decided she would have to get a job, but because she didn't have any training or experience outside her home, she could only get a low-paying job and found that after-school care, clothes, and transportation expenses would eat up her wages. She was crying when she phoned and asked her friend Jessica to pray for her.

"Maybe there's something else you could do," Jessica suggested.

"Like what?" Molly asked. "Hire out as a maid?"

"Well," Jessica encouraged, "You're an excellent cook. You know how to plan the best-tasting, inexpensive meals I've ever eaten. Maybe you could do some catering or something."

Molly couldn't forget Jessica's suggestion. Doing something from her home seemed an ideal solution. She'd still be there for the children and to drive Todd to his daily therapy sessions. A few days later, she'd conceived a plan. She knew there were a lot of women in her neighborhood and church who were employed outside their homes. Wouldn't it be nice, she thought, if one or two nights a week they could put a good, home-cooked meal on the table without having to shop and prepare it themselves. She phoned several women she knew and asked what they thought of the idea. They were enthusiastic. Molly made up a month's worth of sample menus to use as an order form and showed it to dozens of women. Even the "stay at homes" said they'd use a home-cooking service at times.

But there was a risk involved. To get started in her business venture, Molly had to file for a license, upgrade some of her cooking equipment, and buy materials. That would take about two thousand dollars; almost half of her and

Todd's savings. What if she used the money and wasn't able to turn a profit or at least recoup the original investment? They could be worse off than before.

Todd was totally supportive. He even offered to clean vegetables or ice cakes, to do what he could to help from his wheelchair. The children said they would keep up the rest of the house and help with cleaning up and delivery.

That was eight years ago. Molly now runs a business that employs sixteen people. She is working toward a master's degree in nutrition, as well as studying accounting. All three of her children plan to become partners in their mother's lucrative, unique catering firm.

Molly reshaped her entire life for the better by taking a risk. She tapped potential she never knew she had.

Prepared for the Future

Taking risks also develops independence and prepares you for the future. If you purposely take risks in the daily course of your life, you'll be better prepared to handle the unexpected emergencies and even tragedies that are an inevitable part of life. Nowhere have I seen the value of risk taking more dramatically illustrated than in my own life this past year, and in the lives of other widows I have met. Let me use Loretta as an example. I assure you she is the norm, not the exception.

Loretta had never risked going anywhere without her husband. Now she is terrified to leave the house after dark for fear her house will be burglarized while she is gone or some assailant will be lurking in the bushes and attack her when she returns. She has never driven the freeways or flown alone and so has been almost housebound since his death eight months ago. But Loretta is young—only forty-nine years old. She needs to job hunt, which may mean driving halfway across the county in the Los Angeles area.

She needs to go places with friends, but she can't always expect them to pick her up. She needs to get out of the house, which is filled with constant reminders of her loss. Her inability to be alone and independent has added to her grief and kept her from rebuilding her life. Now, she has no choice but to risk going alone or to vegetate.

Kate, another widow, used to take great pride in the fact that, as a dutiful Christian wife, she never risked making a decision without consulting her husband first. A year and a half after his death she admits, "He was my security blanket. If *I* didn't decide, *I* couldn't be blamed if something went wrong. Then suddenly I was overwhelmed by decisions that had to be made: how to invest money for income, whether or not to sell the house, how to transfer titles, which car to buy, whether to put a new roof on the house or repair the old one, and hardest of all, I had to finish raising Jen and Dan (who were fourteen and sixteen at the time) by myself. I had to decide how late they could stay out, how much allowance to give them, whether to make them take summer jobs or to vacation as a family as we always had. I had to decide which colleges they should apply for and which I could afford. For the first few months I threw up every time I was forced to make a decision. One time I wrote my options on little pieces of paper, then closed my eyes and picked one."

Kate told me she desperately wishes she had risked being more independent about making decisions while her husband was alive. She learned the hard way that life is full of unexpected risks over which we have no control. Each of you will be at times faced with situations where you have no one but yourself and the Lord to rely on. If you purposely take risks in the daily course of your life, you are better prepared to handle those that come to you as an inevitable part of life. Taking risks boosts self-esteem because when you step out on untried ground, you accomplish more; you grow, learn, and see yourself as a capable, adequate individual who can keep going despite the odds. Your life will be richer, as you learn to trust others and disclose yourself to them and you'll be one step closer to becoming God's special woman.

Workshop

Becoming Vulnerable

I. The following workshop will help you assess how willing you are to disclose yourself to others. Check the answer that most closely resembles what you would do in each situation.

1. Your best friend tells you she can't have lunch with you because she's busy; then you see her eating in a restaurant with a mutual friend. Would you
   a) Get angry because she lied to you, and stop speaking to her?
   b) Assume she meant she was going to be busy having lunch and say nothing?
   c) Tell her you were surprised when you saw her having lunch with someone?

2. While you're talking with friends, one of them tells a story about a mutual acquaintance that is full of misinformation. Would you
   a) Ignore the errors and say nothing?
   b) Interrupt and add what you know while she's relating the incident?
   c) Wait until she's finished; say that's not what you heard, then tell what you know?

3. You and your husband (or boyfriend) are having serious problems. Would you
   a) Ignore them and hope they go away?
   b) Confide in a close friend?
   c) Talk them over with your husband (boyfriend) no matter how angry or upset he might get?

4. Your neighbor borrows your expensive ski jacket and when she returns it, you discover a rip under the arm and a grease spot on the sleeve. Would you

a) Repair the rip yourself, take the jacket to the cleaners, and say nothing?

b) Next time you see her casually mention the rip and the grease spot and hope she offers to fix the jacket?

c) Show her the jacket as soon as possible and ask her please to have it cleaned and repaired?

5. During the dinner conversation at a family barbecue, your cousin is stating some political opinions that you think are wrong and ridiculous. Would you

a) Keep quiet and say nothing?

b) Comment about your cousin's conversation to your husband on the way home and share your opinions with him?

c) Share your opinions with the group as soon as your cousin stops talking?

6. A woman you serve with on a committee at your child's school starts talking to you about religion and says she thinks there are many ways to find God. Would you

a) Keep quiet and say nothing?

b) Tell her what church you go to and invite her to come to Bible study sometime?

c) Share the Gospel with her?

7. You write a beautiful poem expressing your reaction to a sunset and the beauty of God's creation. Would you

a) Not let anyone read it?

b) Let a few close friends read it?

c) Be willing to have it printed in the church newsletter?

Now, go back and evaluate your answers. a) answers mean you would not disclose yourself at all. b) answers indicate you share only when you think it is safe to communicate yourself to others. c) answers mean you are willing to risk disclosing yourself.

Next analyze every a) or b) answer. *Why* were you afraid to disclose yourself fully? Using the chart below, list your reasons for not disclosing and what risk or fear you perceived.

Reason	Feared result of risk

Part IV

Establishing
a Self-Identity

Chapter Nine

————— • —————

This Is Me!

Let's reflect for a moment on what we've discovered so far. We've learned that good feelings don't just happen—they come and go, depending on what you see when you look into the mirror of self. We've discovered that self-esteem is a variable; that it ebbs if you do not constantly weed out feelings of inadequacy and inferiority and that it grows and stabilizes when you cultivate qualities that produce good, healthy, realistic feelings. Ultimately, your self-esteem formulates the person you become, or your self-identity.

When I taught a seminar in Seattle, I had the privilege of getting to know the program chairperson, Jeannie McCullough. Jeannie, a pastor's wife whose husband is a district superintendent for the Church of the Nazarene, is a warm sensitive, wise, self-assured woman who obviously knows herself well. During dinner, when we were discussing some of the problems that plague Christian women today, the topic of self-worth automatically wormed its way into our conversation. Jeannie, who at that time did not know I was writing this book, told me about a situation that happened in her life years ago that made her realize the importance of establishing an identity apart from her role as wife, pastor's wife, mother, daughter, and sister.

Her husband went from pastoring a church into administration, which involved tearing up roots and moving their family clear across the country. He had to travel a lot in his new position which, in many ways, made Jeannie a single parent to her children, who were five and seven at the time. "I was moving from a comfortable role I was accustomed to into a new phase of life where I felt out of place. I was not comfortable with my surroundings. All of my support systems were gone.

"As I was evaluating where I was coming from and where I was now, I discovered that I had lived my life like I had been sitting in a tiny boat on this nice, placid lake where I was sheltered and everything and everyone that was important to me was within eye distance, sitting on the shore. It was a very comfortable, safe place to be.

"Now, suddenly I was drifting out into the open sea, with no boundaries or familiar sights to guide me. When I'd been on the lake in my tiny boat, I hadn't paid much attention to my oars, but when I drifted into new surroundings, I realized my oars had all been on one side of the boat. My life was unbalanced. And you know what happens when you try to row a boat with the oars all on one side—you end up going around in circles, getting nowhere.

"My oars were my husband, my children, and my church. Although I always had a good sense of self, my identity had gotten so wrapped up in others that when we moved, suddenly it was gone! I realized then that you must maintain a self-identity to survive wherever you are, to know where you are coming from and where you are going, and to be the person God wants you to be."

Jeannie also made another important discovery at that

time. "I realized that it was my relationship with the Lord that gave me my basic identity. I could have sat around feeling sorry for myself because I was isolated from my family and friends, and my husband wasn't around much, but instead, I immediately got involved in the church. I started serving the Lord, not because I was a pastor's wife, but because I loved Him. *He* became what I needed. He gave me my identity. I saw that I'll always have myself as long as I have the Lord."

The next step toward becoming God's special woman is the one Jeannie took: establishing a self-identity; a you who stands alone and apart; a person you can point to and say, "This is me."

The Importance of Self-Identity

There are many reasons why you need a self-identity. One is that you cannot survive without it. Many times, you are all you have. You are the only person you can turn to. In a human sense, you become your only resource; there is no one available to help you but yourself.

Another reason self-identity is important is that self is an expression of our God-created individuality. Paul wrote that "We are His workmanship, created in Christ Jesus for good works, which God prepared beforehand, that we should walk in them" (Ephesians 2:10). I think many Christians visualize the route to heaven as a huge freeway, marked "roadway of faith and service," crammed nose-to-nose with one immense mass of nondescript men and women who all believe alike, think alike, feel alike, and act alike.

Actually, God has paved the road to eternity with separate, distinct pathways for each of His children to follow. Each route is different from any other, prepared by God so we can walk in the way He designed and express ourselves as individuals who possess a unique identity called self.

The Source of Your Self-Identity

God is the foundation of your self-identity. He is a part of you and you are a part of Him. Unbelievers are related to Him in the sense that they are His creatures and He is their Creator. Believers are related to Him as family: He is our Father, we are His children. For me, being a Christian is the most formulative, directional factor of my self-identity. Everything I think, say, and do is predicated on the fact that I am God's child. The words I write, the lessons I teach, every decision I make, my performance as a wife, mother, friend, employee, and even the way I respond to strangers, are all influenced by the all-encompassing truth that I am a Christian.

Self-Identity Stems From Others

But God isn't the only source of your self-identity. The way your life intertwines with others also affects the person you become. The effect others have on you can be good or bad, edifying or debilitating. If someone reflects negative or erroneous images, and you accept them, you lose part of your true identity. If someone reflects positive, correct images, you gain a deeper sense of who you are. For example, I was listening to a Christian call-in radio program, when a young woman phoned for advice. She said she had recently become engaged to a boy she had dated for over a year and that ever since she got her ring, he'd been on her case about everything.

"He criticizes the way I sweep the kitchen floor, walk, comb my hair, and laugh. He tells me what to do, then accuses me of not being submissive if I disagree with what he asks. Then last night, when he was over, I was repairing my oven door. I'm good at mechanical things and he isn't, but he started bossing me around and telling me I was doing it all wrong. And when I told him I wasn't, he got really mad and grabbed the screwdriver out of my hand and tried to fix the door himself. When he couldn't, I did, and he left in a huff, screaming at me that I had put him down and embarrassed him."

Then she said, "I don't understand what's happened. Now he says he doesn't want to marry me unless I'm willing to learn to be submissive. I've never thought of myself as a stubborn person. Now he's telling me I am and it's like I don't know who I am anymore."

The talk-show host assured her that the problem was her fiancé's, not hers. As they talked, he cautioned her not to lose her identity by believing the man's unfounded, irrational accusations. But there was no doubt that his input was detracting from her self-identity.

Conversely, positive input from others can help you establish your self-identity. The mother who encourages her children to ask questions and think creatively; the husband who solicits his wife's opinion and acts on her counsel; the friend who trusts another with a confidence; the business associate who compliments a co-worker on a job well done, are all telling people something about who they are. Such reflections become part of your self-identity.

Author Eric Hoffer noted, "However much we guard ourselves against it, we tend to shape ourselves in the image others have of us. It is not so much the example of others we imitate, as the reflections of ourselves in their eyes and the echo of ourselves in their words" ("Points to Ponder," *Reader's Digest*, November, 1981).

The people who are closest to you have the most profound effect on your self-identity. Anytime you give of yourself to someone, you become a part of that person. In intimate, ongoing relationships, such as parenthood or marriage, your children and your mate actually *are* a part of you and your identity. There is a portion of me in each of my children—genes, chromosomes, values, hopes, dreams, and the love I share with them. In marriage, Scripture teaches that a man and a woman literally become one flesh. They mystically merge into a single entity, while at the same time maintaining their individuality. Being married doesn't mean you are no longer yourself but that you also become part of another person.

Through the years I have taught about the paradox and beauty of the one-flesh relationship, but I never fully understood its depth until George died. I did not just lose my husband—part of me is gone and can never be replaced. I do not know exactly how to describe it other than that certain facets of my personality and the major framework of my life are missing. There is a dark, empty vacuum in my body and soul. I feel as if I had major surgery, a huge portion of my vital organs removed, and the wound left open.

When you lose an important relationship, especially one that contributes to your sense of well-being and self-esteem, as my marriage did to me, you lose an enormous portion of your identity. My identity as George Berry's wife, lover, friend, counselor, and companion no longer exists. It is gone and I will never get it back, but I am still me. While George's death caused me much heartbreak and unhappiness and left me questioning my sense of purpose, this loss did not take away my self-identity. There is still a me who stands alone because I learned many years ago the danger of being so completely submerged in another person that you cannot survive without him or her. It is part of God's plan that each of you develop an identity of your own, apart from anything and anyone but Him.

I cannot tell you how grateful I am that I have always maintained friendships of my own, above and beyond couples who are George's and my mutual friends. I thank God every day that I have a career that forces me to use my mind, occupies my thoughts, and gives me a way to contribute to the lives of others in meaningful ways, as well as providing income. I'm glad that I always reserved a part of me for myself; that I was Jo Berry as well as Mrs. George Berry or Brenda, Cathy, and Brian's mother. Had I not, I would presently be totally incapacitated. My self-identity has saved my sanity. I could not have survived this tremendous loss without a sense of self.

The secret to becoming God's special woman is to become a person in your own right without shutting out others or defying God's authority and charge over your life. Females have to work harder at this than men. Studies show that men generally acquire their identity from their jobs or various status positions they hold, and from exercising their individuality. Women, on the other hand, derive their identity from associations and roles; their families, husbands, children, and friends. Men are known by what they do and who they are; women are known by who they belong to. Yet, our need for self-identity is as real and pronounced as that of our male counterparts.

Every woman, young or old, single or married, needs to establish a self-identity. In his book *Mere Morality*, Lewis B. Smedes validates our desire for self: "Every living thing is kept alive with a vital power to become what it was meant to be. A bush is restless until it produces a rose. A woman is restless until she becomes a whole self, at peace with her own being" (Eerdmans, 1983, pp. 50, 51). Let's look at how to do that.

Workshop

This Is Me!

I. This exercise will help you assess how others affect your self-identity. On the chart, write the names of five people who significantly affect your self-identity and explain how each contributes to it. Include both positives and negatives.

	Person	Contribution
1.		
2.		
3.		
4.		
5.		

II. Pretend you have to give a speech to a group of strangers telling about yourself. But, you cannot tell them what you *do*—your profession, your marital status, your family. You are to describe who you *are*. The purpose of your "This Is Me" speech is to help them get to know you as a person; what makes you tick, your philosophy of life, your likes and dislikes, pet peeves, strengths and weaknesses, talents. On a separate sheet of paper, write your "This Is Me" speech.

Chapter Ten

What Do You Need?

Now let's explore some constructive ways to establish a self-identity. One is to *identify your needs and devise ways to meet them.* Because we women derive most of our identity from relationships and roles, we automatically rely on others to identify and meet our needs. In my opinion, that is why so many women are unfulfilled. Authors Marcia Lass-well and Norman Lobsenz observe, "Most people are not clearly aware of their needs or wishes, much less able to put them into words. Some believe that [others] ought to be able to sense such things: 'If you love me, you'd know what I need.' ... But love does not automatically make one a skilled mind reader" (*Styles of Loving*, Ballantine, 1981).

I remember when George and I were first married I expected him to be able to tell when I wanted to go out to dinner. If he loves me, I reasoned, he will know when I'm too tired to cook or when I feel like having a romantic rendezvous over steak and lobster at a beachfront restaurant.

Then I'd get mad and pout when he didn't offer to take me out. The problem was, George had no way of knowing what I wanted if I didn't tell him.

The truth is, most people can't identify their own needs, let alone the needs of others. Frequently when I teach self-image seminars, I ask the women in the audience to write three of their most pressing personal needs. A majority draw a blank. The last time I did that exercise one woman started laughing and said, "Good grief. I'm always talking about what I want but I haven't the vaguest idea of what I need."

Some needs are general and obvious, such as the need to love and be loved, for food when you are hungry, water when you are thirsty, rest when you are tired, warmth when you are cold, companionship when you are lonely, or freedom from pain when you are hurting. But many of your more intimate, specific needs aren't easy to label. I suggest that you use what I call the "3-R Procedure" to help you identify and meet your needs.

The 3-R Procedure

First, *Recognize* your needs. Call them by their right name. (You'll get a chance to do this in the workshop at the end of this chapter.) You may think you need more time when what you actually need is to restructure your priorities. Jill thought that she needed her husband to show her he loved her, but when she would tell him that, he'd say, "Hey, I come home every night after work, I earn a good living, I give you and the children everything I can, I go to church with you, I'm faithful." From his perspective, he *was* showing love.

Actually, what Jill needed was a little romance. She needed her husband to give her a big hug and kiss when he came home, to put his arm around her shoulder when they were watching television, to hold her hand when they were walking.

Once she recognized that her need was for physical displays of affection, she was ready for "R" number two: becoming *Responsible* to fulfill those needs. Whatever your need, whether simple or complex, you must be willing to take the initiative in solving it. If you need time, you can't expect an extra hour or two to magically appear during the day. You'll have to evaluate your priorities, decide what activities to eliminate, and plan how to use your time more efficiently.

In Jill's case, she started snuggling up to her husband every chance she got. She gave him a big kiss in return for his obligatory peck on the cheek and started holding his hand or laying her head on his shoulder. Now they are a very affectionate couple.

Frequently women are quite passive about meeting their own needs. That's because they operate on the misconception that someone else is supposed to make them happy. Shock waves reverberated through a local congregation when the wife of an elder left her husband. Her reason? "He doesn't make me happy anymore." In reality, no one can make anyone else happy. Others can contribute to or detract from your happiness but they cannot create or destroy it. Gladis and Gordon DePree wrote, "We are sustained by the love of God and the love of those around us, but the quality of our lives can only be decided by each one of us, individually" (*Catch a Red Leaf*, Zondervan, 1980, p. 55).

The fact that each of us is responsible for our own happiness is difficult for most people to accept because we've been conditioned to believe the opposite. We've been taught that parents are supposed to make their children happy, teachers are supposed to please their students, and husbands or wives are supposed to make their mates happy.

So instead of looking for ways to make others happy or taking responsibility for our own well-being, we look for the "happiness handouts" we've been told to expect in our me-centered society. But we find out too soon that others cannot, or do not, or will not make us happy.

Taking responsibility for your own happiness frees you from such expectations and makes you happier because you suffer few disappointments. When you become responsible for your own happiness, you do not feel let down or un-loved when others fail you. You become more your own person.

Neither should you rely on circumstances to make you happy. Instead, you should be actively involved in whatever happens in your life, however pleasant or unpleasant it may be. That's what Angela did in the investigation after she was raped. The rape was extremely difficult for her because she is an unmarried, Christian woman who had never had intercourse. But instead of recoiling in horror, or denying all of the injustice, indignity, and rage she was experiencing, she decided to become as involved in the investigation and healing process as possible. She kept a journal detailing all of the procedures the police and hospital personnel used, and recorded her reactions and feelings every day. She phoned the rape crisis center and joined a support group. She sought spiritual counsel from her pastor because she had a lot of unanswered questions, starting with, "Why did God let this happen to me?"

Angela survived the trauma of rape with a minimum of unhappiness because she decided to participate fully in the ordeal she was going through. We do not have to depend on our circumstances to make us happy. Rather, as someone put it, true happiness can be "the mental state of content-ment which comes from successful adaptation to the world as it really is."

Put on a Happy Face

Another way to become responsible for your own happiness and to meet your needs is to start thinking of yourself as a happy person. To do that, you may have to brainwash yourself a little. First, change your mental image. Whenever you picture yourself as depressed or sad, mentally draw a smile on your face and erase the frown.

Second, be cheerful, even if you feel like an unhappy grouch. When I was a high-school senior, I was an unhappy young woman. I had lost both of my parents within two years, was living in an intense, abusive situation, was terribly frightened and insecure, and felt unwanted and unloved. Then my English teacher, Maxine Kirshbaum, literally forced me to take the lead role in the senior play. I played a happy-go-lucky, slightly wacky woman (could this be typecasting?) who was engaged to the town's most eligible but b-o-r-i-n-g and ever-so-proper bachelor. Her life was turned upside down when she was unexpectedly saddled with raising four younger brothers and sisters when their parents were killed.

I discovered that getting into the character I was playing actually made me happier, so I started pretending I was like her all the time. In a matter of weeks, my depression had lifted, my sense of humor returned, and life was a lot more fun. I was permanently "into" the part by the time the play ended its run.

Third, to think of yourself as happy, start smiling. Follow the advice of the old song and smile, even if your heart is breaking. Greet everyone with a smile. Smile at the multitude of minor mishaps that happen throughout each day. (It *is* useless to cry over spilled milk, so why not try smiling instead?) Smile when you feel like yelling, or frowning, or crying.

Recent research shows that smiling can actually help you develop an identity as a happy person. An article in the *Los*

Angeles Times on May 29, 1985, headlined: "Putting on a
Happy Face: It Works, Researcher Says." Times staff writer
David G. Savage reported, "Putting on a face, whether of
fear, anger or amusement, triggers a genuine emotional reaction in the body, a University of California researcher reported.

" 'We know that if you have an emotion, it shows on your
face. Now we've shown it goes the other way too,' said Paul
Ekman, a professor of psychiatry at UC San Francisco. 'You
become what you put on your face . . . a happy face can in-
deed produce a happy body.' "

A fourth way to start thinking of yourself as a happy person is to do what happy people do. Walk with a bounce.
Hold your shoulders straight. Sing, whistle, or hum while
you work. Savor little pleasures, such as the sight of a rose
or the taste of fresh-baked bread.

Fifth, count your blessings *every time* you start thinking
you are unhappy. Name them aloud as a praise to the Lord,
even if you can't think of many or they seem inconsequential compared to the problems that are plaguing you.

Rely on the Lord

But remember, you don't have to try to meet your needs
alone. You can have God's help. That brings us to the third
"R" in identifying and meeting needs, which is to *Rely* on
the Lord. One of the most comforting certainties about
being a Christian woman is the knowledge that you do not
have to rely solely on human relationships to make you feel
loved and wanted, to attain identity, or to meet your God-
created feminine needs. Accepting that you are responsible
to recognize and respond to your own needs keeps you
from expecting too much of others and teaches you to rely
more fully on the Lord, who promises to "supply *all* your
needs according to His riches in glory in Christ Jesus" (Philippians 4:19).

God is able to meet all of your needs because He knows exactly what they are and has the resources to satisfy them. He can compensate for every lack in any human relationship if you rely on Him. He is the perfect parent; a heavenly Father who dispenses love, justice, mercy, and discipline and who always has your best interests at heart. He has promised to be "a father of the fatherless . . ." (Psalms 68:5).

He is the perfect friend. He is totally trustworthy. Jesus said, "Greater love has no one than this, that one lay down his life for his friends" (John 15:13), then proved His loyalty on the cross at Calvary. He understands you better than you understand yourself. He is always nearby, ready to offer you a shoulder to cry on or to rejoice with you. He is ever sensitive and responsive to your problems, pain, and the longings of your heart. "For we do not have a high priest who cannot sympathize with our weaknesses, but one who has been tempted in all things as we are, yet without sin" (Hebrews 4:15). Because Christ is that kind of friend, you have the assurance that you can "draw near with confidence to the throne of grace, that we may receive mercy and may find grace to help in time of need" (Hebrews 4:16).

The Lord is also the perfect husband. Collectively and individually Christians are the Bride of Christ, ". . . the wife of the Lamb" (Revelation 21:9). Isaiah declared, "For your husband is your Maker, Whose name is the Lord of hosts . . ." (Isaiah 54:5). Whether you are single, widowed, divorced, or married, Jesus Christ can supply every need that is not being met in a marriage. You can lavish your love on Him and be loved *unconditionally* in return. You can worship, serve, and adore Him; give yourself totally and freely to Him, seek His counsel when you need advice, and trust Him to protect and provide for you, as any devoted husband would. Relying on the Lord is the simplest and surest way to identify and meet your needs.

Workshop

What Do You Need?

I. This exercise will help you identify your needs and devise ways to meet them. On the chart, list five present needs in your life; then write one thing you can do to start meeting each need.

	Need	Action
1.		
2.		
3.		
4.		
5.		

II. This exercise will help you see how relying on the Lord can help you identify and meet your needs. Psalm 139 outlines how the Lord shows us we are special by loving us, giving us a sense of belonging, and meeting specific feminine needs. Reach each Scripture, then tell one way God can meet that need in your life.

Verses 1–4: The need to be understood _____

_____

Verses 3, 17, 18: The need for intimacy _____

_____

Verses 5, 6: The need for protection and security _____

_____

Verses 7–10: The need for companionship _____

_____

Verses 11, 12: The need for emotional stability and peace of mind _____

_____

Chapter Eleven

Developing Survival Skills

Identifying and meeting your needs helps you develop your self-identity because it teaches you that you *can* rely on yourself. It also stimulates latent inner resources so you can develop survival skills, another must for establishing a sense of self.

An old proverb warns that you should never place all of your eggs in one basket. If you do, you run the risk of breaking all of them if you fall, and ending up with no eggs at all. Likewise, no adult should ever depend so much on any one person, job, or role that he or she cannot function without it. You should not put all of your eggs in one basket.

Children are by nature totally dependent on others for their survival, but should be nurtured toward independence. Every man, woman, and young person should be able to do whatever is necessary to feed, clothe, and care for his or her basic, life-sustaining needs. Everyone should learn, as early as possible, how to cook a meal, write a check, do laundry, change a fuse or a faucet washer, put out a fire, and give basic first aid. Science-fiction writer Robert A. Heinlein aptly said, "A human being should be able to change a diaper, plan an invasion, butcher a hog, conn a ship, design a building, write a sonnet, balance accounts, build a wall, set a bone, comfort the dying, take orders, give orders, cooperate, act alone, pitch manure, solve equations, analyze a new problem, program a computer, cook a tasty meal, fight efficiently, die gallantly. Specialization is for insects." (*The Notebooks of Lazarus Long*, Putnam).

I recently read about an eleven-year-old boy who got separated from his family when they were camping and was lost in the forest for five days. Although he had no food and wasn't wearing a jacket, and temperatures dropped to below freezing every night, he survived with only a few scratches and bruises because he had developed survival skills. He said he did what his dad had taught him to do if he ever got lost: Don't panic and stay put. He found a sheltered spot, rationed the water in his canteen—ten sips a day—and made a bed of pine needles and dry leaves, which he buried himself in at night to keep warm.

We all need such skills. In today's society, I believe every woman, out of common sense and necessity, should cultivate some means of supporting herself financially, above and beyond her husband's income. I have seen women devastated and left destitute by divorce or the death of a mate; left with children to support, forced to sell their homes, drop to poverty levels of living, or go on welfare or take handouts from aging parents or friends and other family members, because they had no way to generate income. I have seen widows who, after devoting years to marriage and family, have nothing constructive to do with their time if their husbands die or their children leave the nest. They feel useless and worthless. As one woman said, "I can only go to so many luncheons, play so many games of tennis, watch so many television shows, make so many phone calls to friends, visit so many relatives. Then what?"

I am not suggesting that all women have to actively pursue careers or work outside of their homes. I am urging that each of you have something you could do to make money and survive physically and emotionally if you were left alone and had to take care of yourself and your family. Take courses at night school or a local junior college. Learn how to type and operate a computer; to do bookkeeping and speedwriting. Constance, whose husband is a college professor, edited and typed papers for students in her spare time and eventually set up a students' secretarial service and research center on campus. Sally, who loves children and was actively involved in a preschool co-op play group when her children were young, opened a day-care center in her home and, after ten years, got a degree in early childhood education and now owns and operates a preschool. Dorothy did volunteer work at a hospital one day a week. Now she's a licensed practical nurse and is studying for her R.N.

For years, every time one of her friends wanted a special dessert, they asked Barbara to make her famous blueberry cheesecake. Now Barb has a business that nets close to thirty thousand dollars a year. All she makes is cheesecake. She started by having some business cards printed, asking her friends to recommend her to their friends or ogranizations to which they belonged, and by passing out free samples of her goodies in cookware and cutlery stores in malls.

Developing survival skills helps you establish your identity as a capable, competent woman who can do "it" herself, or at least knows how to go about getting it done. Such skills are a security blanket that keeps you from losing your identity when you lose certain roles or when your responsibilities shift.

Become an Independent Thinker

Let's examine some essential survival skills. One is to *become an independent thinker*. My daughter Brenda and I were browsing through the mall when we witnessed a most interesting encounter. A young woman, who looked to be about twenty-five, was shopping with her husband. She'd pick an item off the rack, and he would immediately approve or reject it. He disliked a print skirt she particularly liked. She said, "Well, I'm going to try it on anyway. Maybe when you see it on me, you'll like it better."

He shrugged his shoulders and said, "I wouldn't care to be seen with you if you were wearing it, but try it on if you like."

When she went into the dressing room, he stood outside. She came out and modeled every item for him; then he told her what to buy and what to discard. When she appeared in the print skirt, he said, "I told you it wouldn't look good." Then he handed her one he had selected and said, "Here, this will look much better on you." She didn't buy the skirt *she* liked.

No woman can establish a self-identity unless she learns to think for herself. When you let others tell you what to believe, you reflect their taste and ideas and you get lost in the process. It is my personal opinion that women in general have not been taught or encouraged to think for themselves or to develop their own system of beliefs. Instead, we've been conditioned not to question authority but to accept secondhand opinions as our own. In the Christian community women are told that disagreeing with their husbands, or pastor, or anyone who is in authority, is being "nonsubmissive."

Letting others think for you can be dangerous because you frequently receive conflicting information, which confuses you instead of clarifying your course of action. For example, I have to buy a car. This is something George and I always did together. Now, I have no choice but to do it on my own. I have to laugh whenever I sift through all of the advice I've already received. Whenever I mention that I'll be buying a car, everyone is ready to tell me which brand and model to get. Of course, they all think I should buy the kind they drive. Brian wants me to get a sporty-looking one with a hot engine. My neighbor across the street thinks I should get an American model; my next-door neighbor recommends I buy a Japanese brand. One of George's engineer friends has dozens of reasons why I should buy the kind he bought.

What to do? What to do? If I acted on all of the advice I've received, I'd have to have a car custom-made. So, I made a list of what *I* want in *my* car—cost, availability of parts, cost of repairs, warranties, economy, style, and color. Now I am collecting brochures on the models *I* want to investigate. Then I intend to talk with my mechanic before I buy, because he's the best auto expert I know.

Everyone has an idea about what you should do and how you should do it. Everyone thinks her way is best. A Danish proverb warns, "He who builds according to every man's advice will have a crooked house." You need to think for yourself if you're going to develop a *self*-identity.

How to Think for Yourself

To become an independent thinker, first you must *search out all sides of an issue,* regardless of what you presently believe. Validate facts and discover the truth for yourself. Don't take anyone else's word without first investigating a matter and don't limit your thinking by clinging to what you already believe. Exploring various points of view does not necessarily mean you will alter your beliefs, but you will expand your vision, update information, and gain new knowledge, as well as affirming what you believe and why you believe it. Becoming an independent thinker doesn't mean you do not listen to others or respect their opinions. It means that you accept responsibility for the decisions you make and do not let yourself be unduly influenced by outside sources or past opinions.

As an example, I am presently researching a theological stand about communion. I was always taught and have always believed that the bread and grape juice (or wine, depending on your denomination) symbolize Christ's body and blood. This is a common interpretation, but recently I have met Christians who take a different stand. They believe that the communion elements literally become the body and blood of Christ when we partake of them. They offer the Lord's own words as proof: "And while they were eating, Jesus took *some* bread, and after blessing, He broke it and gave *it* to the disciples and said, 'Take, eat; this is My body,' And when He had taken a cup and given thanks, He gave *it* to them saying, 'Drink from it, all of you; for this is My blood of the covenant, which is poured out for many for forgiveness of sins' " (Matthew 26:26–28). They claim that we should interpret this Scripture as literally as we do the rest of the Bible.

I have never investigated either side of this issue; I always accepted the one that was handed to me as a child and adhered to in the churches I attended. Now, I have been challenged to rethink my belief.

Second, to think for yourself, you must learn to *trust your judgment.* Decide for yourself what is good for you, what is the best course of action, what makes the most sense, what will bring the best and desired results, then go for it. Don't be swayed by what someone says if you are convinced you are right. Trust yourself, your thinking, your motives, and your emotions.

I remember a time when I was discipling a young woman who had to make a major decision about her marriage. Her husband, who was not a Christian, was an alcoholic and for numerous reasons she feared their relationship had deteriorated beyond the point of no return. She was aware that she had such a poor self-image that she had let him, and her mother, and her children, and certain friends victimize and intimidate her for many years. As a result, she had no faith in her ability to make the right decision, so she did what I call "counsel hopping." She asked *everyone's* opinion: her pastor, several Christian counselors, her therapy group, assorted friends, Bible teachers. Of course, she received all sorts of conflicting counsel, which only confused her more. One week she was determined to ask her husband to leave, the next she wasn't; one moment she was convinced the situation was hopeless, the next she was sure they could salvage their marriage. She alternately blamed his drinking and her lack of understanding for their problems. She was on an emotional merry-go-round.

Finally, I was so frustrated for her I said, "Ellen, there's no way you can please everyone or take everyone's advice. You've tried that, and it doesn't work." I suggested she forget everything everyone had told her and that she ask the Lord what she should do. (There I was, advising her not to accept advice from anyone.)

A few days later she phoned and told me she had decided to stay with her husband. When she'd taken time to think and pray through the situation on her own, she had realized they had a lot going for them. I was as excited as she when she told me how she'd gotten the courage to make that decision *and* feel good about it. She said that when she started praying, she told the Lord that she knew she wasn't capable of making good decisions, then she asked Him to tell her what to do. Instead of giving her a specific answer, she told me the Lord spoke to her heart and said, "Ellen, you have a good mind. Use it." She was amazed and delighted. "Can you imagine?" she exclaimed. "God thinks I have a good mind and that I'm capable of making decisions!"

Third, to become an independent thinker, you must be willing to *stand alone.* That's what independence is all about. Be tenacious. Take your view instead of the popular one. Risk seeming offbeat or odd. Martin Luther said, "Every man must do two things alone: he must do his own believing, and his own dying." When you stand alone and have the courage to do your own believing, you catch a vision of your individuality, which helps you establish your self-identity.

Workshop

Developing Survival Skills

I. Are you an independent thinker or are you unduly influenced by the opinions of others? Under each topic, in column A write what you consider to be common public opinion. In column B, write what a person whose opinion you respect believes. In column C write your interpretation of what Scripture teaches. In column D write what *you personally believe.*

Topic	(A) Public opinion	(B) Other person	(C) Bible	(D) Me
1. Abortion				
2. Interracial marriage				
3. Drinking				
4. Smoking				
5. Prayer in schools				
6. Capital punishment				
7. Submission				

What do your answers imply about how much you are influenced by each of the factors?

Chapter Twelve

Becoming Self-Sufficient

Independent thinking leads to another identity builder and essential survival skill—*self-sufficiency*. As a Christian, you should, of course, always rely on the Lord and seek His counsel, direction, and will, but in a human sense, you should rely on yourself first. Generally, women do just the opposite because we've been trained to rely on others. In our society, boys are supposed to be curious, girls compliant. Boys are taught to "tough it out" when the going gets rough and to figure out what to do without asking for help; girls are taught to ask for assistance instead of working through a problem on their own. So, by the time we're adults, we've come to depend on others more than men do, so are not as self-sufficient as our male counterparts.

I saw this when I taught school. The boys seldom asked for help, even when they needed it, but the girls would run to me with all sorts of petty questions they could just as easily have figured out on their own. This same attitude prevails in marriage and parenting. We see it in the wife who won't make a move without her husband's permission or approval and in the mother who uses the old, ineffective wait-till-your-father-gets-home tactic.

The problem with overrelying on others is that they are not always there when you need them. Sometimes you have only yourself. And, depending too much on others debilitates your identity and keeps you from growing. Samuel Smiles acknowledged the importance of self-sufficiency in his essay, "Self-Help," which he penned in 1859! He said, "The spirit of self-help is the root of all genuine growth in the individual . . . help from without is often enfeebling in its effects, but help from within invariably invigorates."

Many Christians balk at the idea of a woman's becoming self-sufficient because they think it clashes with the Lord's charge to be submissive. Often, as I reflect on my own life, I am amused and amazed at how God has literally forced me to rely on myself. I was orphaned at fourteen, with no means of support after high school, no one to ask for advice or assistance, even though I desperately wanted and needed to. Later, the Lord blessed me with a husband who was a devout family man, but one who encouraged me to be a person in my own right. George also traveled a great deal in his work, so I had to learn to be self-sufficient within the boundaries of my marriage. God used those absences to preserve my individuality and to prepare me for the future.

Now I am once again in a situation that is almost identical to that of my teen years—widowed at fifty-two, no longer able to ask my wise, loving, and loyal husband, friend, and counselor for assistance or advice. Certainly the Lord is with me, but in a human sense, I have no one to rely on but myself. I cannot, based on my experience, accept that God does not want each of us to be self-sufficient when He has structured my entire life to tutor me in that process.

How to Become Self-Sufficient

As I analyzed my situation, I recognized four ways God has helped me become self-sufficient. The first is, *become your own primary resource.* No one has all the answers or knows how to do everything. Being your own primary resource doesn't mean you try to do everything alone but that you know where to turn for help if you need it. I can change a washer in the faucet or climb onto the roof and reset the TV antenna when the wind blows it askew, but I could not repair the water main that broke in the front yard. I did have the name of a trustworthy, reliable plumber. I knew how to take care of the problem even though I couldn't fix the water pipe myself.

Being your own primary resource means you look upward—follow James's advice and ask the Lord for wisdom. Then you look inward—appropriate the power of the Holy Spirit. Then you look outward and do whatever is necessary.

Second, to become self-sufficient, *try to do things yourself before you ask for help.* For example, my clothes dryer stopped running. My first reaction was to call for repairs but instead I consulted the service manual and did what it said. First, I checked the fuse. It was okay. Then I pulled the dryer out from the wall, unplugged it, removed the front panel, then vacuumed the motor, oiled the fan, and greased the bearings. Guess what! It's running again. I don't know which pleased me most; the fact that I fixed it myself or that I saved fifty dollars.

Third, to become self-sufficient, purposely *spend time alone.* I know this isn't easy. We all have so many demands on our time, but it is vital to establishing a self-identity because it gives you a chance to make friends with yourself, to enjoy your own company, to get to know yourself better, and to overcome the fear of being alone.

By spending time alone, I don't mean grabbing a few minutes of quiet time every day, although that is necessary, too. I mean removing yourself from the support systems you depend on to reinforce your identity. Instead of going to lunch and shopping with a friend, go alone. Browse the stores. Decide for yourself if something looks good on you or not. Relax when you eat lunch. People watch. Talk to the Lord. Reflect on some of the issues in your life. You don't always have to be with someone to have fun!

I also think every woman should learn to travel alone. You need to know how to make plane reservations, get to and from the airport, make your way through an airport and switch planes, and how to rebook missed flights. You also need to know how to plan and take an auto trip. My friend Jan thinks nothing of piling her three kids in the van and driving from Seattle to Los Angeles. She says if she waited until her husband could go, she would never get to visit her family there.

Eloise and Hugh had been married forty-two years when he died. They were inseparable and used to brag that the only time they had spent a night apart was when she was in the hospital delivering a baby. A few months after Hugh died, Eloise decided she had to get away. She needed a break from everything and everybody. So she took a three-week, sight-seeing motor trip, *by herself!* She said, "When I started, I was terrified. I had never vacationed alone, and Hugh always drove. But once I was on my way, I felt more at peace with myself than I had in weeks. I got up when I wanted and went to bed when I wanted. I wasn't accountable to anyone. If I didn't feel like eating alone, I'd ask some other woman or older couple if I could join them. I made a lot of new friends and met a lot of interesting people. Most important of all, I found out that there is a difference between being alone and being lonely. I had a great time with myself."

Fourth, you become self-sufficient by *doing some things simply because you want to,* beyond duty and the demands of your roles. This will help you develop your individual uniqueness, bring you a great deal of personal satisfaction and happiness, and establish your self-identity. I think of my friend Peggy, a brilliant woman, mother of eight, a professional Christian counselor who is working on her doctorate in theology. Her life is intense, to say the least. Recently, on what she calls a Spirit-prompted urge, she started sketching and painting to relax. "I know this was from the Lord because, let me tell you, I couldn't draw a straight line before," she laughs.

People started raving about her artwork when they saw her drawings. A patron of the arts "accidentally" saw one of them, showed it to a gallery owner, and now Peggy is preparing to display her work at a show. "I can't tell you how fulfilled I feel," she smiled. "This is something that is strictly me, apart from the rest of my life and the people in it; something I do just because I want to."

It is not God's plan that you lose yourself in others, but that you enrich them with your presence and bless them with your individuality. You'll never be self-sufficient if you always sublimate your desires to those of your husband, children, or friends. Each of you needs to set and pursue personal goals that relate exclusively to you as an individual, above and beyond any goals you might have as a spouse, parent, friend, or in your work. This helps you identify yourself as a woman who is separate and special from all others; a capable person in your own right—one of God's special women.

Friends, Friends, Friends

A fifth essential for establishing self-identity is to *have a wide circle of friends.* By that, I do not mean you must have a lot of friends but rather many different kinds of friends from various religious, ethnic, professional, and social backgrounds; friends who are entirely your own, not merely the mutual friends you make as a couple with your husband or acquire by default, like the parents of your children's friends, classmates, or teammates. These private friendships will endure after the kids leave home or if you should lose a mate.

Sadly, many women stifle their self-identity by narrowing their circle of friends once they are married. Men do not. They still go bowling, fishing, and to sporting events with their buddies, but women tend to let such relationships dwindle after they say "I do." In the book *Smart Women, Foolish Choices* (Clarkson N. Potter, 1985), Dr. Connell Cowan observes, "It's always surprising to me how quickly a woman will put aside her female friends when a man enters her life. Yet these relationships are some of the most honest and fulfilling she has. A woman must retain her individuality, her friendships, her interests—in a word, her identity."

No matter how young or old you are, having friends of all ages enhances your sense of self. Those who are older lend wisdom and perspective and give you a sense of roots, stability, and an appreciation of life.

You can find great comfort and joy with friends of your own age. Peers in the truest sense, most of us have "come into our own," are comfortable with ourselves and one another, can accept each other just as we are, without judging or demanding anything of one another. There seems to be a mutual give-and-take between friends of the same age, and few, if any, unrealistic expectations.

Friends who are younger perch you on the refreshing edge of childlikeness and keep you from growing old mentally or becoming too set in your ways. They challenge you with fresh ideas and a different approach to life and its problems. They lift your self-worth as they turn to you for guidance and instruction.

Friends help you establish your self-identity because each of them reflects you to yourself in a different way, exposing you to various facets of your unique personal nature. They help you learn about yourself. They are the sandpaper God uses to smooth the rough edges of your personality so you can conform more closely to Christ.

Self-identity, like self-image and self-esteem, is a variable. Every day you grow. Every experience causes you to see yourself differently, generates new feelings, and alters your concept of self. Every relationship changes you in some way. None of us is the same person she was yesterday. Your self-identity isn't something you ever completely establish; it is whoever you are at any given moment, and the woman you are becoming.

Workshop

Becoming Self-Sufficient

This exercise will help you assess your survival skills and develop self-sufficiency. Read the list. Put an A by each skill where you are adequately prepared, an S by each skill where you are somewhat prepared, and a U by each skill where you are unprepared. For each S or U write a sentence telling what you need to do to start developing that skill.

Safety and First Aid
1. Know location of and how to shut off gas main to dwelling.
2. Know location of fuse box or circuit-breaker box and how to reset or shut off.
3. Know location of and how to shut off water main to dwelling.
4. Know how to put out a grease fire.
5. Know how to stop bleeding.
6. Know how to give CPR.
7. Know how to treat a burn.
8. Know how to treat someone who is in shock.
9. Know how to treat someone who is having a convulsion.
10. Know how to treat a high fever.
11. Know the phone number of police and all emergency services.
12. Know what to do in case of an animal bite.
13. Know what to do if someone takes poison or an overdose of medicine.
14. Know how to treat a drowning victim.

Maintenance
1. Know how to check the oil, battery, and tires on the car.

2. Know how to change a faucet washer.
3. Know how to balance a checkbook.
4. Know how to make a bank deposit or withdrawal.
5. Know how to write a check.
6. Know how to fertilize the lawn.
7. Know how to type.
8. Know how to self-serve gas.

"Need to Knows"

Put a check by each of the following you know. If you are married, you should also know the same data about your husband.

1. The identification number of all of your charge accounts.
2. The identification number of your checking account.
3. The current balance of your checking account.
4. Social Security numbers.
5. Employee identification numbers.
6. Driver's license numbers.
7. The place and amount of all outstanding loans, including mortgage, auto loans, and all charge accounts.
8. The location, identification number, and balance of all savings accounts, IRAs, and other savings plans and investment accounts.
9. The location and number of your safety-deposit box.
10. The location of yours, your husband's, and your children's birth certificates, marriage certificate, military records, school records, and any other vital papers.
11. The name, identification number, and location of all insurance policies.
12. Phone numbers of your husband at work, children's school, family doctor.

Survival

Complete the following sentence: If I lost every means of financial suport, this is what I could do to earn money for myself and my family:

_____

_____

_____

_____

_____

_____

_____

Part V

———◆———

Self-Actualization: Becoming God's Special Woman

Chapter Thirteen

―――◆◆―――

Getting God's Input Through Prayer

Your whole life is a quest for self-actualization—an unending process of *becoming*. You can never assume you've arrived, only that you're moving toward God's ideal. Your self-image improves as you acknowledge and accept that you are made in the image of God, endowed with the beauty of Jesus, and clothed in His righteousness. Your self-esteem rises when you realize that you are of infinite value to God; that He proved your worth by first loving you, even when you did not love Him and could not love yourself. You establish your self-identity as you celebrate your God-created individuality and, at the same time, relate more closely to Him. But you'll never be all God meant you to be, become His special woman, or reach that spiritual, emotional, and psychological plateau called self-actualization without God's input.

You get God's input through His written Word, the Bible,

and through His spoken word, prayer. First, let's explore how prayer can help you become self-actualized. Dr. Alex Carrel, a Nobel-prize winner in physiology, observed that, "... prayer is indispensable to the fullest development of personality." That's because praying puts you in touch with your Creator, who is ideally equipped to interpret you to yourself. I watched a television interview with a man who invented a piece of exercise equipment that monitors heart rate, blood pressure, and various other vital body functions while it's being used. He explained exactly how the complicated, computerized machine works in such simple, concise terms that even I understood. It was obvious he knew every detail about its structure and the way it should function, because he invented it. When you pray, the Lord, who created you, is able to reveal you to yourself and show you how to fully develop your personality because He knows every detail about your structure and the way you should function.

You do, of course, learn some truth about yourself from others, especially from those who love you most and are closest to you. For example, patience has never been one of my virtues, but instead of admitting how impatient I am and trying to change, I deceived myself by saying I was energetic and hated to waste time. So for years the Lord tried to teach me the truth: that impatience was one of my worst faults. One way He did this was through my children. I vividly remember an incident when He used Cathy, who was about nine years old at the time, to convict me. We were stuck in a long line at the supermarket. When I kept snapping at her for no reason, she said, "Mommy, how come you always get mad at me when you have to wait in line?" Ouch! Truth, from the mouth of my child.

God certainly reveals truth to you from those who know you best. He uses your spouse, if you'll listen, and who but the Lord knows you better? He uses friends and sometimes, strangers. Just last Sunday, through the sermon of a visiting pastor I'd never met or heard before, the Lord showed me I was worrying about a minor problem instead of trusting Him to solve it. God's resources are limitless; He can use any person or circumstance to help you discover yourself, but the best and simplest way to attain self-actualization is to ask God directly for His views of your faults and virtues. You should rely on Him, not others, as your initial and most reliable source of input. No woman can discover herself or become God's special woman without calling upon the Lord in truth. When you do, you can expect an answer because "the Lord is near to all who call upon Him, To all who call upon Him in truth" (Psalms 145:18).

Praying Improves Self-Image

I believe that praying, which is conversing at an intimate level with God, can do more to improve your self-image than self-analysis, counseling, or therapy ever could. It is the gentlest, surest way to learn the truth about yourself. Hearing the truth from others sometimes is painful or embarrassing. Sometimes their criticisms, though true and well-intended, come packaged in harsh attitudes and tied with unkind words. But "the Lord longs to be gracious to you and ... waits on high to have compassion on you" (Isaiah 30:18).

We've already discussed how praying improves self-image because it exposes the image detractor of sin and provides a way to eradicate it. Someone said, "Prayer is a receptacle for sin." When you pray, you can toss all of your faults and flaws in God's wastebasket and trust Him to dispose of the rubbish.

Praying improves self-image because it washes the dirt of sin from your soul, so you can see yourself realistically. A few years ago, when I taught a retreat in the mountains, I had a difficult time applying my makeup because the mirror in my cabin was so dirty. I tried washing it but that didn't help because dust had seeped in through tiny hairline cracks and embedded itself in the glass. The dirt distorted my image and kept me from seeing myself clearly. Sin distorts our self-image in the same way, but when we pray, God removes the dirt so we can see ourselves in the light of His truth.

Praying Develops Understanding

Another reason praying improves your self-image is that it helps you understand yourself. Thomas à Kempis prayed, "Send forth Thy light and truth ... for I am ... empty and void till Thou enlightenest me." Each of you needs to be enlightened about yourself by God. Many times you misunderstand yourself. You unjustly judge and criticize yourself. Which of you hasn't called yourself idiotic or stupid at one time or another, or told yourself that something you did was unforgivable, or wondered how in the world you could have done such a foolish thing? We all say things to ourselves and think evil about ourselves that God doesn't think and would never say.

God never misinterprets the truth or misjudges you. His assessments are always fair and correct. "... The judgments of the Lord are true; they are righteous altogether" (Psalms 19:9). When you consult and converse with the Lord, His infallible input helps you develop a proper understanding of who you are and what makes you tick, so gradually you learn to evaluate and accept yourself as He does, in a godly manner.

Praying Affirms Your Worth

Praying also improves your self-image because it affirms your worth. Women who feel worthless are convinced down deep in their souls there is something terribly wrong with them that they are powerless to change and that something is lacking in them that they cannot identify or fill. When you pray, God unleashes His power within you, so you change. He fills you so completely with Himself that His presence, His knowledge, and His will displace those lacks. You feel better about yourself. You recognize you're worth something after all. Your self-esteem rises.

Also, praying improves your self-image because when you pray you see God values you so much that He is eager to lavish His energy, wisdom, and love on you. From a human perspective, I know I am valuable to people when they are willing to spend time with me, talk with me, and show concern for my welfare. When someone phones to see how I'm feeling, she's saying my happiness matters to her. When my children fuss over me when I'm sick, they're saying that my well-being is important to them. When a friend invites me to dinner or asks me to spend the evening with her, she's saying I'm a worthwhile companion. When someone talks with me or confides in me, she's saying that my opinion matters. Communication and contact affirm your worth.

Similarly, communication and contact with God affirm your worth. You know you are valuable to God because He is willing to converse with and listen to you, not just collectively, but individually. As you see Him moving in your life, in response to your prayers, you will realize how concerned He is for your welfare and how much you matter to Him. His attention makes you feel better about yourself.

Praying for Yourself

The reaction that automatically follows when I teach that you should pray for yourself usually is astonishment, surprise, or disbelief. During the prayer time at a Bible study I teach, I asked the women to break into small groups to pray. First, I asked them to take a few moments to share requests. Then I suggested that each woman pray for the person directly to her left, then for the woman on her right. In closing, I said, "Now I want you to pray silently for yourselves. Thank God for something you like about yourself; then pray specifically for one thing you'd like Him to help you change or overcome." Despite the attitude of prayer in the room, one woman popped up and said, "What a great idea! I've never thought of praying for myself."

In my experience, hers is a common reaction. Not many Christians pray for themselves. They pray to receive things, to alter circumstances, for help with problems, or they intercede for others, but very few talk with the Lord about themselves. But praying for oneself is not a unique concept. Scripture is peppered with examples of saints who did just that. Many of the Psalms are "self" prayers. In Psalm 51 alone we read, "Be gracious to me," "cleanse me," "purify me," "wash me," "make me know wisdom," "make me to hear joy and gladness," "create in me," "restore to me," "sustain me," and "deliver me." Solomon prayed for wisdom. Hannah said, "I want to be a mother." Jesus prayed for Himself in Gethsemane.

Praying for yourself is as valid and necessary as praying for others. Think about why you pray for others. Many times you ask the Lord to reveal His will or to show someone the truth about themselves. Just this week I've prayed with a wife who asked God to show her husband how unfairly he's treating their son, with a mother who asked God to show her daughter how deeply she was being affected by her worldly friends, and with a secretary who asked the Lord to show her boss why asking her to lie to his wife to cover an affair he's having with a fellow employee, is unfair and manipulative.

Why should I feel any less justified in asking God to

show me similar truths about myself? You cannot learn the truth unless you ask. God speaks to your heart when you pray, then uses the Holy Spirit, whom Jesus called the Spirit of Truth, to guide you into all truth. (*See* John 16:13.) The question isn't *should* you pray for yourself, but *how* should you pray?

How to Pray for Yourself

Searching the Scriptures, I've discovered five prerequisites for learning the truth about oneself through prayer. *You must want to know the truth.* You must, as David said, ". . . desire truth in the innermost being" (Psalms 51:6).

The second prerequisite is *you must understand what prayer is.* I think of prayer as having two phases: conversing and contemplating. When we pray, we communicate with God. Good communication involves both talking and listening. Too often when we pray, we do all the talking and expect God to do all the listening. We're so busy telling Him what we think He should do that we don't take time to hear what He has to say to us. Because I'm such a poor listener, I developed a technique that revolutionized my prayer life. When I kneel before the throne of grace, I make it a habit to listen before I speak. I ask the Lord what He has to say to me before I start talking to Him. Consequently, I do a lot more listening than I do jabbering.

Quality conversation involves much more than exchanging words. In his book *Caring Enough to Confront,* David Augsburger defined communication as a meeting of meaning. Gladis and Gordon DePree wrote that conversation is "two minds and spirits flowing toward each other; extending, responding, searching . . ." (*Catch a Red Leaf,* Zondervan, 1980, p. 46). What a beautiful picture of what transpires between us and our Lord as we search out His truth through prayer.

Quality conversation also takes time. You must be willing to invest hours, not mere minutes, seeking the truth through prayer. Paul S. Rees noted, "If we are willing to take hours on end to learn to play a piano, or operate a computer, or fly an airplane, it is sheer nonsense for us to imagine that we can learn the high art of getting guidance through communion with the Lord without being willing to set aside time for it."

You cannot periodically rush into God's presence and expect Him to reveal the hidden secrets of your heart. You must quiet your soul so you can hear what He is saying. You need to concentrate on who God is and what message He's conveying. When you pray, you need to remind yourself that you're not chatting with your neighbor across the street; you're experiencing the awesome privilege of communicating with Almighty God. Prayer isn't merely talking at God, to tell Him what you want to be. It is listening to Him, so you can discover what you are and what He would like you to be.

The second phase of praying is contemplating. Ralph Waldo Emerson said, "Prayer is the contemplation of the facts of life from the highest point of view." Contemplating is pondering whatever truth the Lord reveals as you converse with Him, then deciding how to apply it. You must assimilate it into your soul and extract all of the spiritual nutrients, much like your body digests the food you eat. Once you understand that praying is listening and contemplating, as well as talking, you are better equipped to receive the truth about yourself.

Center Your Requests on God

Your requests must be God-centered, not self-centered. When Jesus taught His disciples to pray, the first petition He uttered was, "Thy kingdom come. Thy will be done"

(Matthew 6:10). When He prayed for Himself in Gethsemane, He ended with these words: "Abba! Father! All things are possible for Thee; remove this cup from Me; yet not what I will, but what Thou wilt" (Mark 14:36). Self-centered prayers are filled with "I's"; God-centered prayers overflow with "Thys."

When you pray for yourself, you must follow Christ's example and seek God's will. As I see it, you can legitimately make two basic requests: Lord, show me the truth, and, Lord, conform me to that truth. Then, it is God's voice you hear, it is His face you see, it is His will you seek, as He reveals you to yourself.

Believe God Will Answer

Believe God will answer. It is God's will that you learn the truth about yourself. John assured that ". . . if we ask anything according to his will, he hears us. And if we know that he hears us—whatever we ask—we know that we have what we asked of him" (1 John 5:14, 15 NIV).

You must believe that God listens to and is affected by your sincere prayers and that He wants to reveal the truth to you. You must believe that He wants to help you discover yourself and become self-actualized. You must believe that He affirmatively answers every prayer that is in line with His will. And, you must believe what He tells you. You can't petition for the truth, then reject it because you don't like it.

But God's answers aren't always negative. More often than not He answers in a very positive, affirming way. I remember a time in 1966 when I was doing a lot of soul searching by praying for myself. I was also suffering from severe allergies and migraine headaches that would totally incapacitate me for three and four days at a time. I was taking allergy shots three times a week, as well as a potent pain medication, but nothing seemed to help.

One evening, after I'd been sick with a violent headache for three days, George asked me if I'd like to get out of the house and ride with him while he did an errand. I stayed in the car when he went into a friend's house to deliver some papers. While I was waiting, I started praying. I was halfway convinced that I was having the allergy attacks and head-aches because of some sin in my life that I hadn't pin-pointed. I remember I prayed aloud: "Lord, I truly want to be pure. If there's anything at all that I need to confess or turn over to You, I want to know."

I was expecting Him to reveal some deep, dark, secret sin. Instead, I heard His firm, steady voice say, "Why haven't you given Me your health problems? I want your headaches and allergies."

I laughed because I couldn't imagine anyone wanting them, even God! But I got the message: God's answer was that I wasn't trusting Him with that area of my life. So I said, "Okay, Lord. If You want them, You've got them."

Immediately I was flooded with warmth. My body tingled from head to toe, and I sensed what felt like fingers rubbing my temples and forehead. The headache I'd had for three days was gone.

I've never had another. I never took another shot. Nor have I ever had another allergy attack.

Accept God's Answers

Strange as it may sound, it was several weeks before I could actually believe that God had miraculously, totally healed me. I had difficulty accepting and applying the truth He had shown me. But He used that unique answer to teach me to trust Him more fully.

When you pray for yourself, *you must be willing to accept and apply what God reveals.* Knowledge alone isn't sufficient. You must accept and act on the truth. In my case, I wrote a letter to my allergist, telling him I wouldn't be back for more shots. I told him what happened, exactly as I described it to you. He phoned and asked permission to read my letter at a medical conference in Germany.

I also told everyone I knew that I'd been healed. Even the sceptics couldn't deny that I'd been very sick and now I was very healthy.

Sometimes acting on the truth God reveals through prayer is harder than hearing it. But you cannot attain self-actualization unless you do. When Jesus taught a parable that contrasted a wise person with a foolish one, He said, "Everyone who hears these words of Mine, and acts upon them, may be compared to a wise man . . ." but, "everyone who hears these words of Mine, and does not act on them, will be like a foolish man" (Matthew 7:24, 26). Notice that both men heard Christ's words but only one obeyed them. When God answers your prayers, you are foolish if you do not accept and apply the truth.

There's a favorite slogan among Christians: Prayer changes things. The reason prayer changes things is that prayer changes people. But bowing your head or kneeling or saying pious words isn't what changes you. The condition of your heart is more important than the position of your body. The desire of your heart is more relevant than the words you utter. You must pray correctly and courageously.

Phillips Brooks offered this advice about praying for yourself: "Do not pray for easy lives. Pray to be [a stronger person]. Do not pray for tasks equal to your powers. Pray for powers equal to your tasks! Then the doing of your life shall be no miracle, but *you* shall be a miracle. Every day you will wonder at yourself, at the richness of life that has come to you by the grace of God." You will attain self-actualization and become God's special woman.

Workshop

Getting God's Input Through Prayer

Colossians 1:9–12 is a beautiful intercessory prayer Paul offered on behalf of the Christians in Colossae. In this workshop, you are going to use it as an outline to help you learn to pray for yourself. Read the prayer several times. The requests in that prayer are listed below. After you digest the content of the prayer, complete each sentence, asking God to reveal a specific truth to you in that area. Make very specific requests. Use your responses as a prayer. Take them to the Lord several times a day. When you receive an answer, write another request.

1. *To be filled with the knowledge of God's will.*
Lord, I need to know the truth about Your will for my life in this matter: _____

_____

2. *For all spiritual wisdom.*
Lord, I need to know the truth about the most godly way to handle this matter: _____

_____

3. *For all spiritual understanding.*
Lord, I need to know the truth about why I, a Christian, am thinking, behaving, and feeling in such an ungodly way in this matter: _____

_____

4. *To walk in a manner worthy of the Lord.*
Lord, I need to know the truth about ways I am not walking in a worthy manner in this area of my life: _____

_____

5. *To please the Lord in all respects.*
Lord, I need to know the truth about the things I am doing that displease You in this matter: _____

_____

6. To bear fruit in every good work.
Lord, I need to know the truth about what attitudes and activities are keeping me from bearing fruit in this area of my life: _____

_____

7. To increase in the knowledge of God.
Lord, I need to know the truth about my beliefs concerning this issue: _____

_____

8. To be strengthened with all power.
Lord, I need to know the truth about why I am so weak in this area of my life and what I need to do to appropriate Your power: _____

_____

9. To attain steadfastness and patience.
Lord, I need to know the truth about my level of commitment in this matter: _____

_____

Chapter Fourteen

Getting God's Input Through His Word

Prayer is one way to get God's input. Studying the Bible is another. God's Word is the best self-image book ever written because it has the power to change you. It "... is living and active and sharper than any two-edged sword, and piercing as far as the division of the soul and spirit, of both the joints and marrow, and able to judge the thoughts and intentions of the heart" (Hebrews 4:12) In the Greek the word *active* is "energēs," from which we derive our English word *energy*.

Let me share with you an example of the amazing, transforming power of God's Word. My friend Lue, who lives in Elko, Nevada, told me an amazing story when she was in town for a visit. As we were talking fast and furiously to get caught up on what's going on in each other's lives, she shared that, as one of her many activities, she was teaching a six-month basic Bible-doctrine course to the women in her church. We talked about how exciting it is to see women grow in the Lord as they study His Word and learn about Him.

Then she told me about one woman whose progress had been truly miraculous. This lady, who was in her mid-forties, had been a Chrsitian most of her life, but she was so shy and had so little self-confidence that she had never been able to reach out to others or minister effectively. She felt she had nothing to offer. Lue said, "We could literally see her change as she studied the Word," and by the time the course ended, this woman was a different person. Everyone was amazed at how happy, outgoing, and self-assured she'd become. She was truly transformed and for the first time in her life felt confident and good about herself.

The most significant aspect of this change is that it occurred as she studied the Bible and learned God's truth. This wasn't a course in how to build self-esteem, or how to feel good about yourself or overcome feelings of inferiority or shyness, but *basic Bible doctine!* It covered topics such as who God is, what He is like, the Person of Christ, how to be filled with the Spirit, effective praying, and the meaning of redemption, justification, sanctification, and reconciliation. That woman is a dramatic testimony to the awesome power of God's Word. Without input from it, you cannot become God's special woman.

How God's Word Helps

There are numerous reasons why studying the Bible helps you become self-actualized. It focuses you on the Lord and off of yourself, onto His strength and off of your weakness, onto His immutability and off of your failings. The prophet Jeremiah said, "Thy words were found and I ate them, And Thy words became for me a joy and the delight of my heart . . ." (Jeremiah 15:16). As you consume the

Word and digest its truth, you get to know God better. The more you learn about Him, the more you are able to understand, accept and appreciate yourself, because you are made in His image.

Another reason studying the Word improves self-image is that through God's Word you develop a greater appreciation of life in general. As you discover God's purpose and plan, you realize you are worthy to be part of that plan. You gain a new understanding of what's important and what isn't. You discover that so many of the externals by which you judge your worth are irrelevant and meaningless in God's sight. You learn that treasure in heaven, not money, matters, and that status comes from serving and giving rather than from possessing titles or authority. You are constantly reminded that life is too brief and precious to be wasted, "that we are but dust"; "... just a vapor that appears for a little while and then vanishes away" (Psalms 103:14; James 4:14).

The main reason input from God's Word enhances your self-worth is that through it you learn the truth, not just about yourself, but about God, people, life, and how to solve problems. How does such knowledge help you build better self-worth? By studying Scripture you gain more than information; you learn how to live. For example, if you're having difficulty relating to God (perhaps He seems more like a great overseer in some nebulous place called Heaven instead of a loving Father and close friend), reading the Psalms will show you how David—who was as much a victim of his humanity as we—maintained an intimate relationship with the Lord. Or, the Proverbs offer valuable advice on personal morality and how to behave in interpersonal relationships. Since your self-worth is affected by both your concept of God and your contact with others, such insights about godly living can improve your self-image.

Studying Scripture raises self-esteem because it teaches

you how to survive and to seek sensible solutions to life's problems by using real people, just like yourself, as examples. Watching Mary, the mother of Jesus, at the foot of the cross shows you how to face, accept, and go through the things you cannot change. Ruth teaches us the value of side-stepping selfishness and self-pity. The Samaritan woman illustrates how to overcome sin patterns and rechannel actions and attitudes that detract from self-esteem. From Martha, who like so many of us was "... worried and bothered about so many things" (Luke 10:41), you learn the futility of wasting energy and how to eliminate stress and anxiety. The woman caught in adultery stresses that it is possible to forgive and love yourself no matter what you've done. These scriptural attitudes bolster self-esteem. The more you learn, the better you feel about yourself.

Studying Scripture enhances your self-identity because through it you discover God's will for your life. In some ways, the Bible is like a road map that directs you along the path toward self-actualization and becoming God's special woman. In other ways it is like a mirror that reflects your giftedness and God's concern for you. Through it, you learn the truth about yourself.

The Word of Truth

Jesus said, "... Thy word is truth" (John 17:17). The Bible doesn't just contain truth or tell truth, it *is* truth. All other writings are merely the flawed theories of mortals or human interpretations of God's truth and how to apply it, but the Bible literally is the thoughts, desires, intentions, promises, and character of a Holy God, lovingly reduced to understandable words, phrases, and illustrations for our benefit. Because it was written by God, who is perfect and never makes mistakes, you can trust every word and concept in it. Second Timothy 3:16 declares, "All Scripture is inspired by God. . . ." Every noun, verb, adverb, adjective, preposition, and conjunction in that Holy Book is God-breathed. Therefore, there are no errors or lies in the Bible.

C. H. Spurgeon wrote, "The Bible is a vein of pure gold, unalloyed by quartz or any earthly substance. This is a star without a speck; a sun without a blot; a light without darkness; a moon without paleness; a glory without dimness. O Bible! It cannot be said of any other book that it is perfect and pure; but of thee we can declare all wisdom is gathered up in thee, without particle of folly. This is the judge that ends the strife where wit and wisdom fall. This is the book untainted by any error; but is pure, unalloyed, perfect truth."

Taught by the Author

God doesn't only present His truth in Scripture; He also interprets it to us. When I'm reading a book, especially one that contains complex or difficult concepts, I often wish I could personally ask the author questions or explore a topic more fully with the writer. Frequently I get phone calls or letters asking me to clarify something I wrote or to explain how to apply a specific suggestion. A woman phoned to ask me to interpret something I'd said in one of my books and to help her think through what she should do. Her parting words were, "Talking with you really helped me understand what you meant."

God interprets His writings to you personally. As you read and absorb the content and intent of Scripture, the Holy Spirit of truth "opens the ears of men, And seals their instruction" (Job 33:16). Someone observed, "The Bible is the only textbook which has the author present every time it is studied." God helps you listen, learn, and remember His Word. He uses it to teach you the truth about yourself and improve your self-image. It only makes sense to study His text on self-improvement if you want to become God's special woman.

Studying the Word

Most of us have a very limited idea of study. One misconception Christians nurture is that some people are capable of studying the Bible but others aren't. Let me assure you, there is no such thing as the gift of study! Anyone can do it, *even you!* The problem is that in the Christian community most women are accustomed to learning from secondary sources, such as sermons, Bible classes, tapes, Christian television programs, or Christian books. They rely on others—especially men—to teach and interpret Scripture to them, so assume they are inadequate. Consequently, they never become diligent students of the Word. Be honest. The reason most Christian women don't study the Bible in detail isn't because they don't have the ability; it's because they have never applied themselves to the task.

Becoming a student of the Word requires more perspiration than it does inspiration. You must want to learn the truth about God and yourself badly enough to work at it. In the *Christian Science Monitor*, Nixeon C. Handy told the story of a young man who came to Socrates and said, "I want knowledge."

Socrates replied, "How badly do you want knowledge?"

The young man thought and said, "I must want it badly because I asked."

Then Socrates took him to the beach. When they had waded out up to their necks, he pushed the young man under the water in a ferocious struggle. When he surfaced, Socrates asked, "What did you want most when you were under water?"

"Air! I wanted air!" the young man gasped.

"When you want knowledge like you wanted air under water, then you will get it," Socrates responded.

Similarly, when you want to breathe in more worthwhile feelings of self, you will gasp for a true knowledge of self, as seen from God's perspective, by studying Scripture. When you want to become God's special woman as much as a drowning person wants air, then you will get it.

What Is Study?

Perhaps you've never studied the Bible because you think of study as sitting down with books and drudging through material (a hangover from your school days, perhaps). Study is much more than that. For example, praying is a form of study because you learn as God teaches you through His responses. You learn when you follow the leading of the Spirit and see how He enters and alters circumstances. You learn when you disobey and suffer the consequences of your actions. Study is a way of communicating with the Lord and is one of the best times to listen to Him. I never hear God speak so clearly or eloquently as when He speaks to me through His written Word.

I have always thought of study as having three distinct phases. The first phase is commonly called *devotions*—the personal, intimate time you spend with the Lord. Devotions are not merely devoting fifteen minutes in the morning, praying and reading the current *Daily Bread*. The devotions phase of study is similar to the ongoing love relationship between a husband and wife. It is your "closet" relationship with the Lord. I liken it to the times you sit holding hands with your husband or walk arm in arm, enjoying a sunset. Devotions are spiritual intercourse, when you saturate yourself with Christ's presence and bare your heart and soul to Him.

The second phase of studying is *Bible reading*, which you should do on an ongoing basis to gain a general, overall knowledge of the Scripture and to stay in tune with the Lord. Bible reading helps develop location skills and gain an overview of the events in the Bible, and offers insight into the character of God and how He operates. As you read, God's Word is ingrained into your mind, where the Holy Spirit illuminates the content and stores the information for future use.

Some people like to start in Genesis and read through the Bible each year. That never seemed to work for me. I always got bogged down around Numbers. I've found that a good way to maintain a Bible-reading schedule is to pick a specific book, possibly one you haven't read before or don't know much about, and read it, or a portion of it if it's a long one, every day for a month. At the end of thirty days, you'll know that book. The content will be embedded in your memory. Right now I'm reading through Romans because I'm teaching it. I divided it into fifths and am reading three chapters every day for the next five weeks. As always, I am amazed at the richness of God's Word. I've read and studied Romans several times before, but I'm making many new discoveries.

It's also important to read a portion of one of the Gospels each day because they detail Christ's life and keep us focused on Him.

The third phase of study is actual *study:* laboring in the Word, picking apart passages, searching for hidden meaning, digging to gain in-depth knowledge of the Scriptures. We shouldn't study just to collect facts or to become a spiritual know-it-all. Paul warned that knowledge in and of itself is not valuable, because ". . . Knowledge makes arrogant, but love edifies" (1 Corinthians 8:1). He cautioned Timothy about women who are ". . . always learning and never able to come to the knowledge of the truth" (2 Timothy 3:7). So knowledge for the sake of knowledge is not the goal of study.

Study Techniques

Women frequently tell me they would like to study and they know they should but they don't know how. In her book *The Joy of Discovery in Bible Study*, Oletta Wald shares her similar frustration. "I had been a student of the Bible for several years before I learned how to become a discoverer on my own. I could follow the suggestions of others and answer the questions they asked, but I floundered when I tried to launch out for myself. I did not know where to start or what to do. The treasures of the Bible seemed locked behind abstract words. I always had to depend on someone else to open the door."

Ms. Wald goes on to explain that she was finally able to open that door herself when she learned in seminary how to study the Bible methodically and systematically. Most of us are not seminarians, but we still need to develop some basic study techniques so we can feast on the meat of the Word. The method I'm going to suggest is only one approach. It's the one I use and is a compilation of several methods I've tried over the years.

There's no one way to study the Bible. You will need to experiment to develop a way that works best for you. Once you start studying, you'll probably do as I did and develop a study method that meets your personal needs, but the following ideas should get you going and start you on the way to becoming a Bible student.

Making Time

To study the Bible seriously, you must make time for study. My son, Brian, who is in the tenth grade, sets aside about two hours each day for homework. My friend's daughter, who is in college, studies two hours a day for each course she's taking. Students don't just *take* time for study; they *make* time for it, because it is a priority. Before you do anything else, sit down and plan out your study time. Schedule an hour for it into your day. Be flexible. It doesn't have to be at the same time every day, but it *is* important to study every day. Think of this study time as a self-improvement course you attend daily, which is taught by the Lord. If you can't find an hour a day, perhaps you need to restructure your priorities. How much time do you spend watching television, reading books or magazines, talking on the telephone, or running to meetings? If you are serious about learning the truth about yourself, you'll collect sixty minutes from somewhere.

And to answer that unasked question, yes, I think a full hour is necessary if you want to become a student of the Word. We shouldn't rush into the Lord's presence when we study. This is a time when God converses with us through His Word and His Spirit. What a unique privilege, to be able to open the Holy Book and actually commune with the One who wrote it!

The Translation Dilemma

Next, collect the basic study materials. Obviously, you won't be able to run out and buy all the reference books right away, but you can make use of the ones in your church library or possibly borrow one or two from your pastor. You'll need several translations of the Bible because different translations serve different purposes.

There are three basic types of translations: literal, which is a word-by-word translation from the original language, with the words and phrases kept in the exact order they were written in the original manuscripts; free translation, in which ideas and concepts, rather than words, are translated in context; and paraphrase, in which the ideas and concepts are translated, but some are transcribed in a different order and some are omitted altogether.

Each translation was written for a specific reason. When King James took the throne in 1603, he ordered the development of the King James Version to compete with the Geneva Bible, which was translated by a group of people in England in 1560 who believed commoners should be able to have copies of God's Word in their homes for everyday usage. King James instructed the translators to make the most of the King's English by including as many words as possible. He was more concerned with extolling the beauties of the English language than getting an accurate translation of the Scriptures. So, as popular as it is, the King James Version, which was completed in 1671, is not the most accurate translation, but is an absolute necessity for study because so many concordances are keyed to it.

Most scholars agree that the American Standard Bible (1901) is the most accurate because it is transliterated (translated letter for letter from the original manuscripts) and was done after many more Greek manuscripts had been found. Its updated counterpart, the New American Standard Bible, which is a literal translation, was done in modern language and released in 1963. It is a very accurate translation.

The Revised Standard Version (1946) attempted to translate the American Standard Bible into modern English. Some fundamentalist theologians object to this version because they claim there were stated Communists on the board and that key words referring to Christ's deity or sin are mistranslated or watered down.

The Amplified Bible (1958) is actually a minicommentary that defines words (some that aren't in the original manuscript are inserted) and lists synonyms in context, as well as interpreting the meaning of concepts and phrases. Some Bibles, like the Scofield Reference Bible or the Ryrie Study Bible are basic translations that are embellished with notes that interpret the text according to the scholar's theology.

The Phillips translation, which was completed by J. B. Phillips in 1947, is a popular paraphrase. Phillips believed that the thoughts in Scripture were inspired, but not the words, so translated accordingly.

Good News for Modern Man (Today's English Version) is a free translation that was mass-produced and released by the American Bible Society in 1966 to get inexpensive copies of the New Testament into the hands of the public and introduce them to the Gospel. It is a popular giveaway evangelistic tool but stresses the humanity of Christ rather than His deity and some theologians believe it shows no equality between God the Father and God the Son.

One popular and accurate free translation is the New International Version. The Living Bible, a paraphrase, is the work of Kenneth Taylor, who believes in the literal, word-for-word inspiration of Scripture. It is easy to read and doctrinally sound, but should be used with a study Bible. The New International Version, which is written in paragraph form in modern language, is quite true to the original text and easy to read and understand.

What's amazing is that the truth, power, and purpose of God's Word has endured, despite these, and many other translations. Each can serve a purpose as you study. In their book, *How to Read the Bible for All It's Worth,* Gordon D. Fee and Douglas Stuart recommend using more than one translation. "The sixty-six books of the Protestant Bible were originally written in three different languages ... We assume that most [of you] do not know these languages. That means, therefore, that for you the basic tool for reading and studying the Bible is ... several good English translations."

Your basic Bible library should include a King James

Version, because more concordances are keyed to it. The New American Standard Bible and the New International Version are best for word-for-word accuracy of the text and are written in easy-to-understand modern language. Use the Amplified Bible for depth and detailed meaning of words, a Phillips translation for beauty and flow of the language, The Living Bible for simplicity and clarity of concepts, and a reference Bible for quick, convenient amplification of the text. Fortunately, many of these are available in paperback, or sometimes you can get excellent prices on hardcover editions in used bookstores.

Other Basic Study Materials

Your library also should include a Bible dictionary, a topical Bible, and a concordance. A Bible dictionary gives definitions and some historical or cultural explanation of terms. For example, if you look up the word *parable,* you will find the meaning of that term plus an outline of various kinds of parables and how they are used in Scripture. A topical Bible lists verses and passages topically. If you wanted to do a study about the meaning of *resting in the Lord,* you would look under the heading *rest* and find all of the Scriptures that relate to that subject. A concordance gives the Hebrew and Greek meaning of words, the languages of the original biblical manuscripts.

When possible you should add a Bible atlas and Bible handbook to your study library. An atlas contains maps and geographical information, and a handbook has biblical and historical data, along with information about the cultural backgrounds of nations and people mentioned in the Bible, charts and diagrams, church history, and chronological and genealogical charts.

Eventually you will want to buy two or three commentaries. Because commentaries contain the writer's personal theological interpretation of the Bible, they should not be used as a basis for personal study, but they are good for comparing your opinions with those of the experts and for gaining additional insight into a passage.

Setting Up for Study

Where you study affects the way you study. If you settle into your favorite reclining chair in the family room with your study books stacked on the end table, you won't accomplish much. You need a special area in which to study—a comfortable place that's free from distractions, where you can spread out your materials and not be disturbed or interrupted by room traffic, the television, or the telephone. Of course, a desk is ideal, but a card table set up in the corner of a bedroom will do just as well. The important thing is to set yourself aside and remove as many distractions as possible.

Before you start to study, quiet your heart before the Lord. Confess your sins, pray for the Spirit to teach you, for God to give you wisdom and insight and to reveal the truth to you. Prepare your mind by reading one of the Psalms or a portion of one of the Gospels. You might want to preface your study time with your regular Bible reading.

Expect a reaction as you study. Remember, God's Word is going to cut and pierce your soul with the truth and judge the thoughts and intentions of your heart. E. Stanley Jones said, "Come to the Word expectantly ... surrendering to the truths here revealed ... expecting to use the truths here revealed."

William A. Quayle observed that "the Bible is the Book that holds hearts up to the light as if held against the sun." In the same way, God can make you transparent to yourself as He shines the light of His Word on your soul. He will convict you, expose you to yourself, then bless and restore you.

What to Study

What you study is also important. Usually, I study whatever I'm teaching or writing about—sometimes topically, sometimes through a book. If you've never tried in-depth Bible study before, you might start with some psalms, for they are rich with information about the character of God. Have a purpose for whatever you choose. Don't just randomly pick a chapter or book. If you've always wanted to understand the Old Testament sacrificial system, you might pick Leviticus. If you're interested in the foundational formation of the church, try Acts. If you're having difficulty in some of your interpersonal relationships, you could study Proverbs.

To concentrate on developing self-worth, I've discovered that studying the life of Christ—seeing how He acted and reacted to people, and interacted with them (especially women)—raises self-esteem because you'll understand how important you are to Him. And, studying the lives of people in the Bible improves your self-image. Analyzing their personalities, faults, strengths, and behavior helps you understand and accept yourself, and reassures you that God loves and values you no matter, just as He did the saints of old. Regardless of your purpose for studying, you should decide what you want to learn and why before you begin.

How to Study

Once you've settled into your study area and prepared your heart, it's time to begin. You start by *observing* Scripture. Bible translator Myles Cloverdale advised, "It shall greatly help you to understand Scripture, if you mark not only what is spoken or written, but of whom and to whom, with what words, at what time, where, to what intent, with what circumstances, considering what goes before, and what follows."

When you begin, read the passage you've chosen several times in each of at least three translations. As you read, determine what the passage is about and look for a theme, some overall truth which can be applied and used in a practical way. You might find outlining the passage in paragraph form helpful. Remember, a verse or passage can have more than one key premise. For example, you could view the story of Jesus' meeting with Nicodemus in John 3 as a study of salvation, or of the meaning of the Holy Spirit, or of the scope of God's love, or of the importance of knowing Old Testament Scripture, or of condemnation and judgment—the list goes on. I use it as an example of Jesus' teaching methods when I present teacher-training classes. As you read a passage, trust the Spirit to show you the theme or principle He wants you to pull out.

After you've observed, you're ready to *interpret* in a verse-by-verse, concept-by-concept study. God's method for studying and teaching His Word is outlined in Isaiah 28:10: "For precept must be upon precept, precept upon precept; line upon line, line upon line; here a little, and there a little" (KJV). Don't try to cover a lot of material at one sitting. Take it line by line, idea by idea. Do one verse at a time. Read each verse at least three times, or until you've absorbed the content, underlining important words and ideas as you go. Then write your own interpretation of the meaning of the words you underlined.

Next, look up key words in a concordance or Bible dictionary to absorb the exact meaning. Look up related verses. The Bible is the only Book in the world that is its own cross-reference. Cross-references are usually in the center or side margin of a page. Make sure your Bible has them, as some do not.

When you finish studying a passage, you may want to consult some commentaries for further insight. Don't be disturbed if some of the conclusions you read in the commentaries don't agree with yours. Renowned, intellectually brilliant theologians disagree. Don't think of such discrepancies as right or wrong but as different perceptions about the depth and mystery of God's Word.

Someone said, "The Bible is a mirror in which man sees himself as he is." When you look into Scripture, the image of self God reflects to you is true. But you must be willing to look. When you do, God fulfills His promise that "My Word . . . which goes forth from My mouth . . . shall not return to Me empty, Without accomplishing what I desire, And without succeeding in the matter for which I sent it" (Isaiah 55:11). That promise includes revealing the truth to you so you can develop self-worth God's way and become His special woman.

Workshop

Getting God's Input Through His Word

I. The Word of God serves many purposes in the life of a
believer. Read each Scripture; then answer the question.
   1. Psalms 119:9: How can studying God's Word
help you maintain personal purity? How can it affect
your moral values? How does living a pure life help you
feel good about yourself?

_____

_____

_____

   2. Romans 15:4: How can studying the lives and
personalities of Bible characters help you?

_____

_____

_____

   3. Psalms 19:7–11: This passage lists many benefits
you can derive from knowing and applying God's Word.
First, define each term; then list the attribute that describes it. (You may want to use a dictionary or Bible
dictionary.) Finally, write a benefit it can bring to you
personally. (An example is provided for you.)

Term	Trait	Definition	Benefit
a) The law of the Lord	Sure	Word, teaching	I've been depressed lately and studying God's Word could lift my spirits and restore my soul.
b) The testimony of the Lord			
c) The precepts of the Lord			
d) The commandments of the Lord			
e) The fear of the Lord			
f) The judgments of the Lord			

II. Now you're going to practice studying. First, read Luke 10:38–42 in at least three translations. As you read, note the following:
   1. What is the setting? _____
   2. What is involved? _____
   3. What is happening? _____
   4. What is one overall theme of the passage? _____
   _____

Next, read each verse at least three times. Underline important words and ideas; then list them here and write your own interpretation of the meaning.

Word or Idea	Meaning

Now, look up key words in a concordance or Bible dictionary. Amplify the definition you wrote on the chart above.

Next, look up every cross-reference and decide how it applies to the passage.

Now, on the chart below, do a character sketch of each person in the passage.

Person	Attitudes	Personality traits	Reactions
Jesus			
Martha			
Mary			

Finally, summarize the message this passage held for you.

_____

_____

_____

What did you learn from doing this study that you did not know before?

_____

_____

How do you intend to apply (use) what you learned?

_____

_____

Afterword

We've talked about so many concepts in this book and covered so many important points, perhaps you're feeling a bit overwhelmed. I know that sometimes happens to me. When it does, I find myself asking, "How could I possibly do all of that?" or "What should I do now?" Let me offer a word of encouragement. We've already established that you *can* improve your self-image, cultivate self-esteem, and establish your self-identity. You *can* develop self-worth God's way. But, you must remember that *becoming is a process.* These things won't happen immediately or all at once or in neat, systematic stages. Sometimes you'll progress (grow); other times you'll regress (slip back). What's important is that you not get discouraged and that you keep going—no matter what. Don't give up on yourself. Ever! God doesn't. Neither should you.

Once you commit to developing self-worth God's way, don't try to change everything at once. *Do one thing at a time.* Don't try to go on a diet, quit smoking, start exercising regularly, revamp your wardrobe, stop watching soap operas, become an optimist, and start teaching a Sunday-school class at your church all at the same time. Pick the one thing you most want to change about yourself, which you believe most adversely detracts from your self-worth, and work on it first.

How can you know where to start and what to do first? I advise that you *do what you FEEL you need to do.* Don't try to do what anyone else suggests. For example, Annie asked her best friend, her husband, and her kids what they thought she ought to try to change about herself, and every one of them told her they thought she ought to start working on controlling her temper. But as Annie thought about what she should do, she realized she was harboring a lot of anger and unforgiveness in her heart against her parents, because she thought they slighted her in favor of her older sister. She realized her temper was a symptom of a deeper problem. Once she started developing self-worth by working on her relationship with her parents, her temper subsided, as she dealt with the buried anger and resentment.

You have to decide for yourself what to do. Your feelings are legitimate. When you're seeking God's will, the Holy Spirit activates your emotions and speaks to you through them. You know yourself better than any other person does. Decide what bothers you most about yourself, what will make you like yourself better, and what you want to do to change it—then do it!

Also, *stay in touch with what's happening in your life.* We are all affected by our circumstances. If you're facing problems, whether massive or minor, you may get down on yourself. If you've had a week where every little thing went wrong, from finding a flat tire on the car Monday morning when you were running late, to having the choir director at the church tell you you weren't going to sing the solo in the Christmas cantata this year, you may start feeling poorly about yourself. Not because there's anything wrong with you, but because of what's happening. At times like that, you need to tell yourself, "There's nothing wrong with me." Dislike your circumstances, but don't let your circumstances make you dislike yourself.

Strange as this may sound, *another thing to avoid is trying too hard.* You know what happens when we put undue pressure on ourselves—we blow it! For example, I'm a good cook. I can fix an elaborate dinner for a crowd and draw rave reviews for my culinary efforts. But, for many years, every time we entertained a certain friend, who is a home economics major and gourmet cook, I ruined the dinner. Once I even cooked a tough turkey, and that's hard to do. I know this happened because I was trying too hard instead of relaxing and using my usual dump and stir approach.

It's good to set goals and make plans, but not to burden yourself with them to the point where your self-worth diminishes because you feel incapable or inefficient. The best way to approach your self-improvement project is with an easy-does-it attitude.

As you go about the business of developing self-worth, to keep from getting too wrapped up in yourself, *become an encourager to others.* Every day, offer a smile, an encouraging word, a positive comment to everyone who crosses your path, from the grocery clerk to your kids to the grumpy receptionist in the doctor's office. A positive approach will bolster your self-esteem, as well as theirs.

Finally, *remember that you are already special to the Lord.* You don't have to do anything to win His love and approval. Your motive for becoming God's special woman should be to release and develop the innate specialness He created and planted within you, to bring glory to Himself, blessing to others, and joy and fulfillment to you. You *are* fearfully and wonderfully made. I pray that you, like the psalmist, will soon be able to say, "And my soul knows it very well" (Psalms 139:14).